Coping with Crisis:

A Counselor's Guide to the Restabilization Process

Jim Burtles, KLJ, MMLJ, FBCI

- Helping people overcome the traumatic effects of a major crisis.
- The 4 Stage Restabilization process is explained, in layman's terms.
- Advice is given on how to approach the work, and when and where to offer this particular form of counseling.

EXPLORATIONS IN METAPSYCHOLOGY SERIES

First Edition: September 2007

Library of Congress Cataloging-in-Publication Data

Burtles, Jim, 1935-
  Coping with crisis : a counselor's guide to the restabilization process / Jim Burtles. -- 1st ed.
      p. cm.
  Includes bibliographical references and index.
  ISBN-13: 978-1-932690-41-5 (trade paper : alk. paper)
  ISBN-10: 1-932690-41-7 (trade paper : alk. paper)
  1. Crisis management. 2. Employees--Counseling of. 3. Stress management--Problems, exercises, etc. 4. Emergency management--Psychological aspects. 5. Disasters--Psychological aspects. I. Title. II. Title: Counselor's guide to the restabilization process.
  HD49.B864 2007
  658.3'85--dc22
                                        2007023010

Distributed by:
Baker & Taylor, Ingram Book Group, Quality Books
Published by:
Loving Healing Press
5145 Pontiac Trail
Ann Arbor, MI 48105
USA

http://www.LovingHealing.com or
info@LovingHealing.com
Fax +1 734 663 6861

Loving Healing Press

Explorations in Metapsychology Series:

- *Beyond Trauma: Conversations on Traumatic Incident Reduction, 2nd Edition,* Ed. by Victor R. Volkman
- *Life Skills: Improve the Quality of Your Life with Metapsychology* by Marian K. Volkman
- *Traumatic Incident Reduction: Research & Results,* Ed. by Victor R. Volkman
- *AMI/TIRA Newsletter Vols. 1-2: Selected Reprints 2004-2005 (ISSN 1555-0818)* Ed. By Victor R. Volkman
- *Coping with Crisis: A Counselor's Guide to the Restabilization Process* by Jim Burtles
- *Traumatic Incident Reduction, 2nd Edition* by Gerald French and Chrys Harris

TIR Applications Series:

- *Children and Traumatic Incident Reduction: Creative and Cognitive Approaches,* Ed. by Marian K. Volkman
- *Critical Incident Stress Management and Traumatic Incident Reduction: A Synergistic Approach,* Ed. by Victor R. Volkman

**"To be what we are,
and to become what we are capable of becoming,
is the only end in life"**
—Robert Louis Stevenson (June 1880)

Loving Healing Press is dedicated to producing books about innovative and rapid therapies which redefine what is possible for healing the mind and spirit.

Table of Contents

Table of Figures

Acknowledgements

The search for a way of reducing the personal after-effects of a crisis led me to two major sources of information and help:

Beverly Seligson: A practicing psychotherapist who has specialized in working with people in crisis, she has proved very helpful to me while developing the process described here.

Steve Bisbey (1952-2004): Director of Counseling at the Centre for Applied Metapsychology (East Grinstead, West Sussex), who helped me to make the process easier, both to teach and to learn.

Introduction

BACKGROUND: The author and his environment

For several years, Jim Burtles was Principal Consultant with Safetynet PLC, where he taught business executives how to cope with, and plan for, minor emergencies, disasters and absolute catastrophes. Safetynet was a pioneering disaster recovery and business continuity company which specialized in dealing with business emergencies. Such events might range in scale from a faulty air-conditioning system to the aftermath of major earthquakes or terrorist attacks.

The original concept of Safetynet was centered on the complex computer-based operations of the modern business. However, experience soon taught Safetynet's founders that the whole of the business environment had to be taken into account. Therefore, personnel problems and many other aspects needed to be taken into consideration.

Jim acquired his expertise in disaster recovery and emergency management through direct exposure to dozens of real-life disasters, almost a hundred emergencies and countless problem situations. He also benefited from the indirect experience of many more, gained from talking to, and working with, victims of various crises.

Holder of a Lifetime Achievement award, he is a Founding Fellow and a Board member of the Business Continuity Institute, a Freeman of the City of London and a Knight of Grace within the Military and Hospitaller Order of St. Lazarus of Jerusalem.

In his current role, as a Director of Total Continuity Management, he is now working with senior executives of international corporations and government departments to help them develop complete emergency response plans and processes which include appropriate counseling and training programs to cope with emergency situations.

A Caution about Words and Study

You will only derive benefit from reading this Guide if you actually understand it. While many of the words will be familiar to you, some of them may not be. Words we understand can expand our knowledge and ability and the opposite also holds true: words we do not understand can diminish our knowledge and ability. Sometimes the problem lies in the way the word is being used, perhaps to express an unusual or unfamiliar meaning.

Words used in a specialized manner are defined in the Glossary (beginning on p. 95). Be very careful that you do not go past any word which you do not fully understand.

Bear in mind that many misunderstood words are commonly used, or apparently simple. Some words in common use have a number of meanings, which can vary according to the context, and we do not always have a clear grasp of all of the possible meanings. Don't be too proud to check out the very simplest of words.

Confusion, or the inability to grasp or learn, comes *after* a word that the reader does not have a full and proper definition for. Their attention gets hung up in the mystery surrounding the undefined word.

If the material seems confusing or difficult to grasp, there will be a word you have not understood. Go back to a point *before* you got into difficulty and find the misunderstood word and get it defined. Use a good dictionary and/or the glossary to blow away the confusion.

Preface

The methods described here were originally developed as a means of handling the way people react after a catastrophic event. However, the resultant technique can be very effective in dealing with the aftereffects of almost any traumatic event, whether it is of a catastrophic nature or not. The technique works for any major personal crisis.

Working as a consultant in the field of disaster recovery and emergency management, I perceived the need to find some way of preventing, or alleviating, the emotional disturbance that appeared to be a common result of people being exposed to a major disaster.

It seemed logical to suppose that those who were exposed to less dramatic emergency situations were probably going to be affected in a similar manner; perhaps to a lesser degree, but nevertheless affected. It is my fondest hope that you will find this method to be useful in your own therapy milieu.

1 | Discovery of Emotions

From my observations, there seem to be five common reactions to a severe crisis. I think of these as the "Five Discoveries of Stress'" Four of them are, in effect, a discovery about "oneself in crisis" and the fifth is a kind of discovery of what is regarded as *unknowable*.

They are the discovery of:

- Fear,

- Excitement,

- Capability,

- Chaos, and

- Unknowable Numbness.

Each of these reactions eventually led to similar consequences. The victims distanced themselves from the scene to some extent: mentally, physically, or both. Although not everyone fits neatly into one category or the other, the point is to give us a basis for discussing the most common reactions you are likely to encounter in those who happen to be particularly afflicted.

 ## Discovery of Fear

When people suddenly find that they are unable to control the situation around them, they experience fear of the unknown. Often this perceived inability to control is simply a matter of less control than before. Bear in mind, some of us are not in full control of the scene where we *normally* operate. Most of us have learned to cope with a certain amount of mystery and confusion around us, as part of our regular environment.

This discovery of fear is accompanied by a realization that fear is a most unpleasant or uncomfortable experience. Thus, when things have returned to normal, the subconscious reaction is to regard the once comfortable place of work as a place where life can become most uncomfortable. The victim will seek to change to a safer place of work, one that does not retain the ghosts and shadows of bad memories, or anything which reminds them of those bad memories. Another point worth mentioning is that for many individuals, a repeating pattern begins to emerge and with each repetition they become more firmly locked into the pattern and its effects.

 ## Discovery of Excitement

A very few individuals will react to the crisis in a totally different way. For these, the event seems exciting and dramatic and they enjoy all this random activity around them. When everything is back to normal, these people feel let down and seek further excitement, which they will either create or find. To create it they might in rare cases do something as extreme as setting a fire or they may simply be less cautious, leaving windows and doors open or taking risks in some other way. If they do not create the danger that leads to excitement, they will take up alternative employment in the hope that things might go wrong and hence recreate this feeling elsewhere. What is more, they may subconsciously set out to become a contributory factor to the next "exciting" event. Again a pattern can emerge and become self-perpetuating.

Discovery of Chaos

For many people, who have always led and sought a stable, comfortable lifestyle, their first experience of chaos comes as a rude shock. What they have always feared and avoided has now invaded their own personal territory. Suddenly, they have been confronted by a situation in which there was very little to cling to. Now everything seems to be mobile and insubstantial. All the familiar soothing noises of normal activity, the comforting souvenirs and pictures of the family seem to have been replaced by a noisy whirlwind of activity, in which nothing stays still long enough to become familiar. Next, we'll quickly examine two typical subtypes of chaos response.

"Suddenly there was a deafening silence—nothing can ever be the same again."

After being burgled, many people say they feel invaded and unhappy rather than robbed. They have feelings of guilt—guilty of being a victim!

They will have acquired some new knowledge from this unexpected experience. This new knowledge needs to be evaluated; its intrinsic value and relative truth have to be weighed against existing knowledge. Wherever there is a conflict between existing and new information, the mind will tend to come down heavily in favor of the old knowledge, on the basis that it has proved workable in the past. Even if the old knowledge proved unworkable, at least the degree of unworkability is known and can be allowed for. Familiarity breeds a kind of comfort, which is preferable to the uncertainty always brought about by any significant change. Changes of attitude, viewpoint or behavior are always very difficult; much more difficult than a change of position, location or working environment.

Cognitive dissonance is a psychological term describing the uncomfortable tension that may result from having two conflicting thoughts at the same time, or from engaging in behavior that conflicts with one's beliefs, or from experiencing apparently conflicting phenomena.

In simple terms, it can be the filtering of information that conflicts with what you already believe, in an effort to ignore that information and reinforce your beliefs. In detailed terms, it is the perception of incompatibility between two cognitions, where "cognition" is defined as any element of knowledge, including attitude, emotion, belief, or behavior. The theory of cognitive dissonance states that contradicting cognitions serve as a driving force that compels the mind to acquire or invent new thoughts or beliefs, or to modify existing beliefs, so as to reduce the amount of dissonance (conflict) between cognitions. Experiments have attempted to quantify this hypothetical drive. Some of these have examined how beliefs often change to match behavior when beliefs and behavior are in conflict.

Social psychologist Leon Festinger first proposed the theory in 1957 after the publication of his book *When Prophecy Fails*, observing the counterintuitive belief persistence of members of a UFO doomsday cult and their increased proselytization after the leader's prophecy failed. The failed message of earth's destruction, purportedly sent by aliens to a woman in 1956, became a disconfirmed expectancy that increased dissonance between cognitions, thereby causing most members of the impromptu cult to lessen the dissonance by accepting a new prophecy: that the aliens had instead spared the planet for their sake.

"Better an end with tears than no end at all."

The normal conclusion for this type of person will be, "It is obviously possible to survive chaos, but it is most unpleasant." We all require a certain amount of chaos around us for the sake of learning and to avoid boredom. The problems begin to occur when the amount of chaos exceeds our own personal threshold. Different individuals will have differing degrees of tolerance to disorder or chaos. Clearly, there are those who seem to thrive on chaos and there are those whose well ordered lives are an attempt to limit, or eliminate chaos.

For the latter type of person, the sudden discovery, or perhaps rediscovery, of the effects of chaos will be an unpleasant experience—otherwise they would have been wrong to avoid chaos in the past. The mind will resist all attempts to make it seem to have been wrong. Being wrong is unpalatable and unacceptable to our subconscious mind, it must prove itself to be right—no matter how devious the proof.

Having revisited and reinforced the decision that chaos must be avoided at all costs, this seeker of a stable environment will now see the current situation as potentially unstable and therefore to be avoided. One way of avoiding the place is to get sick; another is to find a new job. An even more effective combination is to get sick *and* find another job. In my experience, this person can be expected to have, at least, a cold or flu after a traumatic event. In the extreme they will even go so far as to get run over by a bus rather than return to the "scene of madness".

Discovery of Capability

When someone is suddenly plunged into a situation where the old rules no longer apply, they are often given, or assume, a higher degree of responsibility. Then they discover their capability to exercise more control, or make decisions, or make things happen or whatever. In short they discover their true worth, or at least get closer to it.

When all the fuss has died down, they are then expected to continue doing the same job as before. Gone is all the excitement and sense of power or control. Feeling deprived their new role, this person now seeks more responsibility and will begin to look elsewhere to find it. In my experience, they are unlikely to apply for promotion or expansion in their current environment; they will automatically assume that where there has been no growth in the past, there will be no growth in the future. This is of course, a perfectly rational and often valid assumption.

Having outgrown their current position, they will be keen to move to a place where they feel they may get the recognition and appreciation they need, want and probably deserve.

Subconsciously, they might not have been fully motivated for some time. They may have felt slightly frustrated with a rather mundane job which held few challenges. This type of person needs to be stretched to feel alive and is often summarized on a personnel report form as "Works well under stress," "Unflappable" or "Capable, but lazy." The last comment reflects a situation where the reporter had not observed the person working happily and purposefully under pressure.

Unknowable Numbness

There is a type of person who is, literally, dumb-struck by a traumatic event. They become petrified with an apparently irrational fear—their fear is far greater than the situation seems to warrant. Their basic under-lying fear is the fear of knowing (or experiencing) the unknown.

It is a fear of being afraid. They have always as-sumed they would be unable to cope in a situation where they were truly afraid. This assumption gets proved right because the person mentally retreats and will not confront the situation they suppose they can-not cope with.

This numbness, of course, reinforces the certainty that their mind cannot cope. As this has happened every time they have been exposed to an unusual situa-tion, the reinforcement has conditioned them to respond with "instant incapability" in the event of a cri-sis.

They will now regard their old working environment as a place that is "too dangerous". They will not feel comfortable there again, unless the place is altered out of all recognition, literally.

Post-Crisis Exit Effect

As we have seen, almost everybody will revise their viewpoint of both the job and its surroundings after ex-periencing a major crisis. For many of them, it will lead, in due course, to a subconscious need to move. This move will be to a new type of work, a new place of work or a combination of both.

Because they are compelled by an unidentified, sub-conscious desire, their conscious mind will need to invent some kind of rational explanation for the urge to seek change. The social veneer level of "thinking" will be saying something like "I feel like a change, don't want to be stuck in a rut" or "Perhaps I should spend more time with my ageing parents, young kids, puppy dog, fishing rod or aunt in Australia." As some of these "excuses" may seem rather weak, they may be consciously restructured to be more acceptable. A whole fabric will be woven around the invented excuse to make it seem more plausible by giving it a complete context. They will soon develop a watertight explanation for themselves.

The end result is a high proportion of the staff resigning for all sorts of apparently unconnected reasons. Much of this subliminal thinking may take weeks to surface and further days, weeks or months to implement. Thus there is such a lag between the true original cause (the crisis) and the eventual consequence (job change) as to disguise the connection. I call this phenomenon the *Delayed Physical Exit*.

Not everyone will respond to their subliminal thinking by a full-scale departure—at least, not on the physical level. For some individuals, these pressures will only cause them to depart from the scene in a mental sense, a large part of their attention will be focused elsewhere. They will while away the hours, and make themselves feel more comfortable, by day-dreaming about their ageing parents, young kids, puppy dog, fishing rod or aunt in Australia. As their mind is not fully on the job they will be more prone to accidents and errors than "normal". I call this the *Delayed Mental Exit* phenomenon.

In effect, these daydreamers are operating (responding and reacting) according to their fantasies almost as much as they are to the realities surrounding them. The more fantasy-oriented they are, the more inappropriate their interpretation of, and reaction to the real world in which they are operating. They have removed themselves from reality as a form of mental protection. This "removal" could be likened to a temporary separation or, in extreme cases, a complete divorce from the real world.

Our fantasies, our private mental universes, have different terms of reference to the normal exterior physical universe. Thus our minds can become attuned to the different pace, differences of importance, different reaction times, different values, morals, ethics, etc. of those other universes. When we need to handle the real physical universe, our reactions are inappropriate, because our mind is operating at the wrong pace, with wrong values, wrong morals etc. The end result is a wrong solution, because the mind is operating with a wrong set of values which are inappropriate for the actual *de facto* situation.

As a result of these two exit effects, a strong team is soon weakened by lack of numbers and a reduced capability. Often these delayed exit effects begin to strike just as the company seems to be on the road to recovery. This second, incipient crisis can be more harmful than the original, obvious event.

I felt that if we could find out how to reduce the impact of these exit effects, it would prove very worthwhile from the business point of view. Obviously, there were many benefits to be gained if we were able to find a means of restoring a person's ability to cope with the challenges of daily life.

Crisis Intervention: Returning People to Normal

The technique described here is directly derived from the Rational Emotive Behavioral Therapy (REBT) model. REBT, developed by the late Albert Ellis, Windy Dryden et. al., is an established and proven way of helping people who are suffering symptoms of depression, anxiety and other issues. One such novel derivative of REBT has been to use it on people who have been exposed to a catastrophe.

In a sense, it can be seen as an emotional "stitch in time." If it is not delivered early enough, the open wound will have become a permanent scar. The mind will have found a method of coping, which involves burying the crisis and its effects beneath a layer of taboo. This layer of taboo is the mind's defenses at work; originally intended as a survival mechanism to prevent unnecessary pain, it is now reducing ability by shutting off the memory and the subsequent learning process.

In the immediate post-crisis period, while the experience is still fresh in the mind, the victim will be willing and able to talk about it. After a few days the survivor will have learned to cope with not talking about it, this then makes it increasingly difficult for them to admit to themselves that something actually did happen. The mind's automatic defense reaction is to pretend nothing happened and avoid contact with anything remotely associated with the event. The event becomes hidden away in the darkest recesses of the mind, where all the other apparently, or seemingly, unconfrontable items are dumped.

Restabilization: a post-crisis recovery process

I have chosen the term *Restabilization* to describe this particular technique in order to convey a sense of what it sets out to achieve. Also, it is a relatively friendly term from the prospective client's point of view. Whenever a group of people is in a position to benefit from Restabilization, they are likely to be fairly sensitive about receiving any form of treatment or therapy, where there may be an implication that they are mentally disturbed.

Restabilization is meant to imply a light, simple pick-me-up that will soon get people back to their normal, sensible selves without any social stigma or long-term dependence. Some people still do hesitate to jump in to any form of what might be regarded as mental treatment. To the casual observer, Restabilization may appear to be reminiscent of Critical Incident Stress Debriefing or CISD as it is commonly referred to. Readers already familiar with CISD may wish to visit Chapter 10 for a comparison.

After a severely traumatic event, people need to be Restabilized. The process I am suggesting is based on the theory of Crisis Intervention. There may be other ways of dealing with the symptoms but this process *does* work, has proved to be effective for many cases, and has no harmful side-effects.

Restabilization should be offered to *all* those who were aware of the crisis, or *trigger event*. Anyone who was linked to the place, the time, the people or the property of the trigger event will have been exposed to the after-effects. It should be made perfectly clear to all those who were exposed that it is completely normal for a person to be thrown off balance by a traumatic event.

The subject of Restabilization should be introduced at a meeting of all those concerned (see Chapter 6).

- *Everyone* should be offered the opportunity

- It should *not* be obligatory

Restabilization should be offered as early as practicable, because delay reduces the effectiveness of the process. A lengthy delay will render the technique completely ineffectual. If the trigger gets stale because of unavoidable delays, one would need to resort to a more highly focused technique, delivered by a qualified counselor.

Ideally, Restabilization should be offered shortly after the event by a skilled counselor, preferably practiced (or at least trained) in this technique. Crisis Intervention is a form of immediate help. It is the provision of help while help is still welcome, rather than offering sympathy after the need has worn off. Crisis Intervention is the counselor imposing control, with the client realizing that control is still possible. This demonstration restores clients' belief in control, and their ability to exercise control.

> If a destabilized person is not
> Restabilized quickly...
> They will stabilize as an unstable,
> Unable or unhappy person!

Further Help

Once the Restabilization process is complete, you will have helped the clients to get back on their feet, restored to the pre-crisis condition. It is also possible they may now feel even better than before, partly because they can compare the way they were beforehand and afterward. Additionally, it is possible the process did something rather more than a simple repair job and actually did make them better than they were before by providing insights.

Because the process has worked and was effective over a relatively short time span, you will have demonstrated to them that they can be helped, they can make progress to overcome effects of traumatic stress. Consequently they may want to try the benefit of more of the same, or something similar.

If they are prepared to consider additional counseling to gain more benefit, we should do what we can to help them with their desire to make further progress. The results of group members seeking further progress and personal growth are also a benefit to all those around them, both at home and at work: something not just socially acceptable but indeed desirable.

Check with the client that they feel OK to ask for more help either now or in the future before you finally send them out to face the world on their own.

The Restabilization Process

There are four basic recovery stages involved in the Restabilization technique, although for a complete understanding of the client's perspective it is necessary to take into account the preceding traumatizing or Trigger Event. The introduction of the counselor (Stage 1) is the effective beginning of the technique, assuming that the counselor is called in as a result of the original crisis. Where it is possible to spot the event before it happens, an entirely different approach might be required. Prevention is much better than cure (see Fig. 2-1, *The 4 Restabilization Stages* on p. 15).

Cognitive Analysis is a standard technique[1] for getting clients to develop understanding of their behavior or reactions and to realize that there is a better solution. By identifying a preferred behavior pattern for themselves, they are more able to cope with such a

---

[1] As used in Rational-Emotive Behavioral Therapy (REBT) practices.

situation in the future, thus they can face the outlook with much more confidence. Restabilization takes this approach a step further and gets the client to rehearse and practice the improved behavior pattern to reinforce and stabilize the benefit. Therefore, clients can gain long term permanent benefits rather than mere temporary relief.

The 4 Restabilization Stages

TRIGGER EVENT		A crisis occurs...
1	**RECAP**	Set up for Cognitive Analysis
2	**REVIEW***	Cognition = understanding the effect(s)
3	**REPAIR***	Analysis = better solutions
4	**REINFORCE**	Recommend & reinforce new solutions

Fig. 2-1: The 4 Restabilization Stages

*Steps 2 & 3 are known as Cognitive Analysis

Fig. 2-2, *Restabilization – An Overview* (see p. 16) is a skeleton that shows how the various session elements fit together and how the overall Restabilization process works.

Restabilization – An Overview

STAGE	QUESTIONS	SESSION GOALS
	CRISIS EVENT	
		Stage 1
RECAP	What happened? How is this event bothering you?	Behavioral description of the event itself and any subsequent reactions.
		Stage 2
REVIEW	Did you anger or upset yourself? How?	Indication of inappropriate thinking relating to the event (realizing the current solution is self-defeating)
Cognitive Analysis		**Stage 3**
REPAIR	What else could you have done to avoid, short circuit or change the solution?	Identification of fresh solutions on 3 levels: A) New Thoughts; B) Identification of new feelings and statements; C) Alternative behavior(s).
		Stage 4
REINFORCE	How do you feel now? How would you solve the problem now? What will you do next time?	Recommendations and the reinforcement of the new feelings and solutions. Practice the new behavior pattern.

Fig. 2-2: Restabilization Overview

Breakthroughs

The Damage of Doubt

"Cynthia" was a highly qualified and experienced trainer who had been successful for a number of years. Apparently her nervousness had driven her to become very knowledgeable about her subject. The ability to answer any obscure question posed by her students gave her a degree of confidence, which enabled her to assume the identity of a competent teacher. She knew her subject and her lessons were carefully prepared; nothing was left to chance. Her competence, and the confidence it generated, were painstakingly constructed but fragile.

During her early thirties she took a break to start a family. When she returned to work as a trainer a year later, she had the misfortunate to meet Derek, a rather overbearing student. This student complained about her attention to detail. Derek said he felt her teaching material was over the top and her style was too wordy. Although Cynthia had used the same material successfully for many years, she amended the materials and modified her style of teaching as a result of this criticism.

Over the next couple of training sessions, she received relatively poor feedback, which caused her to experience severe self-doubt.

During the first Recap session she suddenly realized what she had done: "I've allowed that young so-and-so to destroy my perfectly good way of teaching the subject. I was stupid enough to go into self-destruct mode. Actually I was a very good teacher, and I still am if I stick to my original ways which I worked so hard to develop. Thank you for listening. You've given me back the strength to go back and show off my enthusiasm and knowledge of the subject."

We went though the motions of the rest of the process but her recovery was essentially founded on that one moment of realization.

The Importance of Words

John, a previously bright and successful student became mediocre when he changed to another school. He seemed to experience the most difficulty with mathematics, which had previously been his forte. His mother thought it was strange for him to be struggling with the most logical of subjects where a keen brain should be a distinct advantage.

During the review session, the young man identified a phenomenon, which may have been at the root of some of his difficulties. His new math teacher appeared to be working from a different source of reference. As he said: "This man appears to be using a different language; there are moments when I just don't understand what he is trying to say. Then it takes me a while to catch up with what is going on. I keep finding myself struggling with the subject I used to thoroughly enjoy. If only I could see what he means."

The clue was in the reference to language. During the repair session that followed soon afterward, John came to the conclusion that he might have misunderstood some of the words his teacher had been using. It was possible these words had a special meaning in that context or simply they were unfamiliar. Our young student decided he should get hold of a technical dictionary and check out the meanings of the words which his new teacher was using in connection with mathematics. He was happy to believe that language skills had let him down rather than an inability to deal with the logic of mathematics. Over the next few days he pored over a pile of textbooks and dictionaries.

When he returned for the final reinforcement session, he proudly declared that the problem had more or less vanished when he checked out some of the basic mathematical terms. "Suddenly it all became clear. One moment I was having a hard time reading through a math textbook and a couple of minutes later it all began to flow and I could flip through the pages. I realized I didn't recognize a couple of words, so I looked them up in the two dictionaries I was using and Bingo! I think I'll start using a dictionary to help me with my English lessons."

A couple of months later, his mother reported that he was doing well at school and had even written a few poems to demonstrate his new-found command of, and enthusiasm for, the English language.

Each session stage should have clearly understood goals, which should be closely pursued. Additions and deviations will reduce the effectiveness of this technique.

- Restabilization is not a democratic process.

- The counselor should act in a direct, positive and confident manner when using this technique.

The Trigger Event

The trigger event is any set of circumstances that are sufficiently unusual as to cause abnormal behavior or abnormal reactions. Life is a whole series of such incidents, both at home and at work. Normally a person develops a stratagem, learns how to deal with the incident and adds the solution to their mental toolkit, ready to cope with the future. Whenever someone is overwhelmed by the circumstances, this developing-learning-coping process breaks down. The normal has now become abnormal and we have no stratagem for handling the abnormal. By definition, if we had such a stratagem it would not be an abnormal situation.

What used to be the right way to solve problems has now failed. An argument now intrudes and blocks off all rational thinking: "My way of solving problems does not work. Was I always wrong *or* has the world changed? If I was always wrong, I must cease doing things wrong, i.e., stop doing things in case they are wrong" or "If the world has changed, I don't belong here, *or* I must do nothing until it returns to normal." This confusing dilemma can lead to an *Activity Collapse* or a reduction of the ability to act, think or react effectively.

A crisis can be an opportunity for self-discovery, which may lead to self improvement. This self-discovery and the benefits that might spring from it will only happen if either:

A.   The survivor is unusually objective about the situation, including his/her own reactions and the implications. Such people are able to get involved and yet remain totally objective; they are not subject to the effects of surrounding events. In a few cases, this ability comes out of past successful adaptations to life experiences. (This type of highly resilient person is so rare as to be of theoretical interest only. We must assume nearly all survivors will fall into the other category.)

or

B.   The survivor is led or guided to become objective about the situation, their own reactions and the implications. This second type of person is not able to step back far enough to remain totally objective and control their reactions; they are subject to the effects of surrounding events.

Session #1 – The Recap Session

The primary objective of the first session is to get the client to describe, for themselves, their view of what happened. A secondary objective is to prepare them to look more closely at their reactions, with a view to moving on to consider whether there are any alternative reactions or interpretations of the event.

The event itself is often a fairly obvious happening one can easily refer to as "the fire", "the earthquake" etc. However, this recent incident may only be one of a whole series of occurrences that have built up to form the crisis, from their viewpoint. Get the client to define the scale and scope of the crisis. In order to achieve this, we may have to build toward the complete picture, one step at a time.

A Typical Recap Session

A Recap Session[2] might go something like this:

"I want us to look at what you saw and felt, is that OK?"

"Yes, I do feel I need to talk to someone."

"That's good. Tell me briefly about what happened yesterday."

"Well, my car started to smell funny, and then it caught fire!"

"Really. How did you react to that?"
"Well, as a matter of fact I was very surprised."

"OK. Why did that surprise you?"
"I didn't know cars could catch fire."

"Right. How did you feel about it, at the time?"
"I was a bit scared at first, but then I got angry at the man who sold it to me."

"I see. How do you feel about it, now?
"Still angry and a bit silly for having been scared."

"OK. Was that the beginning of the crisis?"
"No, I seem to have had a lot of things going wrong lately."

"Alright. How long has this been building up?"
"For quite a while now—at least 6 months."

"I see. Can you define the crisis for me?"
"Well, yes I seem to have been angry about other people letting me down or trying to make a profit out of me."

---

[2]In this, and subsequent, examples statements, remarks and comments of the client are *italicized* to distinguish them from the statements, questions and responses of the Counselor.

"OK. Tell me, when did this anger against other people start?"

"Last April, when I bought that old banger."

"Right. How does all this bother you?"

"I feel I'm always being used by other people. Yes, I think that is my basic problem—I object to being used."

"Alright. If we've defined the basic problem, how do you feel about it now?"

"Hmm... I think I am beginning to understand myself a bit better."

"OK, let's just look at today's progress. You told me the car catching fire caused you to feel frightened at first and then you began to feel angry at the man who sold it to you. You traced these feelings back to when you bought the old banger, last April. Then you came to the realization that you don't like being used. You say you are beginning to understand yourself better. Well done. Do you feel you can go out and face the world now?"

"Yes, I feel talking about it has helped."

"That's good. Thank you for talking with me. We'll pick up the discussion on the next appointment."

Sample Recap Questions

The kinds of question the counselor should ask in this first session are those which will elicit the client's reactions to the event and a description of the event from their point of view. Later the questions need to focus on a better understanding of the reactions and their appropriateness.

- "When did the crisis start?"
- "Tell me what happened."
- "How did you feel about that?"
- "How is this event bothering you now?"
- "Have you reacted that way before?"

The counselor should be trying to get the client's perspective. The client might well want to give the "official" or "reported" version of the incident in an effort to please. It is essential they are encouraged to give a self-centered version of the incident and uncover their actual feelings, not what they think they ought to have done, said or felt.

Recap Session Goals

The primary purpose of this first session is to obtain a description of the trigger event in behavioral terms. The person's feelings and experiences are the keys to unlocking the subconscious processes that will enable better self-understanding of the reactions that occurred. This understanding is the basis of recognizing and improving his or her response to the trigger event, and any previous or subsequent similar event.

Session #2 – The Review Session

In this second session, the counselor encourages the client to review the reactions to the event, and recognize the possibility of a better way of reacting. We need to focus on the client's reactions and the reasoning behind them.

The counselor should pick up from the previous Recap Session and the progress which was made at the time. Meanwhile the client may well have evolved a different perspective on the whole thing.

A Typical Review Session

"Last time you said you felt angry when your car caught fire. Why did you get angry?"

"Like I said last time—I feel I get used by other people."

"Fine, good you told me. Does getting angry make a difference?"

"Everyone gets angry when someone lets them down, don't they?"

[The wise counselor doesn't get into a debate about what everyone else does, but simply returns to the line of questioning.]

"Can you use this anger constructively?"

"NO—but I do hate people who get angry."

"So how do you handle that—being angry and yet hating people who get angry?"

"It's natural to get angry when there is a good reason."

"OK. You just said 'I hate people who get angry'. Is there another way you could put that?"

"What I really mean is—I get angry about being angry. You know, I think anger and hatred are more or less the same thing really."

"Good. Is there some other way you could look at this?"

"There is no point in getting angry, it only makes matters worse. Anger seems to make more anger, which makes even more anger."

"Alright, you say there is no point in getting angry because it only makes things worse. How could you avoid that?"

"It's obviously not the best way to react when things don't go smoothly, but it is human nature, isn't it?"

[Again the counselor sticks to the process, avoiding a debate on human nature.]

"OK. Let's look at that reaction, could there be some other way of reacting?"

"No, I mean yes, of course not, I don't have to be angry. That's not the most sensible way to behave. It's quite silly really. I could choose not to be angry, I suppose."

"Fine—have you any idea why it is you react in that manner?"

"Well, yes I think it's because I don't like to be made to feel foolish."

"I see. Is feeling foolish what makes you angry, then?"

"No, I don't think it is the feeling foolish so much as the silly fear of it happening without me realizing it. It's a fear of someone else having some sort of power over me. Stupid of me, really. If I don't react they can't affect me. Wow, now there's a thought!"

The client has gained a better understanding of a basic problem. This needs to be acknowledged. Every answer has to be acknowledged as a part of the cycle of communication (see p. 63). If you fail to respond in this way, the client will eventually begin to feel you do not care or do not hear. Lack of acknowledgment will upset the client and cause them to withdraw from the counselor, the session and the process.

"Very good! What else could you do in this situation?"

"I suppose I could take a deep breath and count to ten. I might punch someone or something or I could swear out loud."

"Good. Can you give me any other possibilities?"
"It's all very silly really, perhaps I should just smile and say nothing about it. Getting angry is a waste of effort and makes me feel unhappy for the rest of the day. Maybe if I was to talk to someone when I get angry, that might help."

"Excellent. You have said that anger and hatred are more or less the same and anger seems to make more anger. Would you agree we have made progress today?"
"Oh yes, I'm feeling a lot brighter about it all now."

"OK, good. Our next session will be next Thursday when we'll look at ways for you to avoid getting angry."

Sample Review Questions

Ideally, the answers should come from the client. You can ask questions like:

- "Do you feel that was the right response?"
- "How else could you have responded?"

Review Session Goals

The counselor is seeking to derive from the client, in response to questions:

- An indication of inappropriate reactions or thought processes, relative to the trigger event;
- An indication that the current 'solution' is self defeating or destructive.

Beware of making the person feel they are, or have been, wrong; they need to find a more successful solution, not a "right" solution to replace a "wrong" solution.

Session #3 – The Repair Session

During the Repair Session, the counselor helps the client to develop better solutions for the future, based on the knowledge gained in the previous two sessions. In the Review Session, the client gained an understanding or cognition which he/she needs to analyze in order to arrive at some new responses or behavior patterns.

A Typical Repair Session

The Repair session picks up from the progress made during the previous Review session and works toward establishing useful solutions for the client.

"We established last time that anger is self-defeating. How could you have avoided getting angry?"

"If I hadn't been frightened, I might not have got so excited about it. The anger was a way of recovering from the fear I guess."

The counselor returns to and pursues the original question, which has not been answered. This is a demonstration of control and is sticking to the process, which requires the alternatives to be considered.

"OK, but how could you have avoided getting angry?"

"Talking to someone would definitely have helped, but there was no-one to talk to. I was alone in the car."

"Fine, you say talking would have helped, but what else could you have done?"

"I don't know; what could I do? I was alone."

"Would listening to someone or something have helped?"

"Oh, you mean the radio or something like that. No, I don't think listening to the radio would have helped. Want I needed was a real person, not another mechanical thing that would let me down. As it was, there was no-one to listen to until afterward. By then it was too late to stop me from getting upset."

"I can understand that. Do you have any other thoughts?"

"Maybe I could just pretend there was someone to listen to; I could recite a poem or something. Yes, that's it I could learn to recite a nice peaceful poem."

"That is a good idea; we need to find the right kind of poem for you. How about using the *Golden Treasury of Verse* as a starting point?"

Sample Repair Questions

The type of question the counselor might use here would be:

- "What could you have done to change the solution?"

- "How could you have avoided getting upset?"

Repair Session Goals

We are seeking the identification of sound solutions on three different levels. The client is now ready to really benefit from the Restabilization process with:

1. New thoughts;
2. New feelings and statements;
3. Alternate behavior pattern(s).

Armed with these benefits, the client will be freer to choose his or her behavior as a conscious choice rather than as a subconscious automatic reaction. The client will be regaining control over self and the environment.

Session #4 – The Reinforcing Session

In this final session, we aim to underpin the Cognitive Analysis. The client needs to rehearse and practice the new solution(s). The aim is for him/her to be able to react in the newly found better manner if another similar event should ever occur.

A Typical Reinforce Session

"We have looked at the original problem, seen how it affected you and thought about better ways of dealing with it. Today, I want us to reinforce what we've learned by putting your new ideas into practice in some imaginary scenarios. Last time you found what seemed to be a good solution. You said you would want to have someone listening but if that was not available you could pretend there was someone there if you heard yourself reciting a poem. Is that a fair summary?"

"Well, more or less. I said I was going to look for what I called a 'nice peaceful poem' and you suggested I might find one in the Golden Treasury."

"That's right. Did you find something you felt you could use?"

"I did look through a couple of poetry books but somehow I didn't relate to other people's words. It all seemed rather impersonal and it was the personal touch that was missing in the first place. I think the basic principle of imagining someone there is fine. I am not afraid of a silent aftermath anymore but learning to recite a poem doesn't seem to be working for the moment. Maybe I need to do some more work in that area."

"OK, I can understand your concern about finding the right material but how does that affect our proposed way of coping with one of these unexpected events? Can you think of a way around the problem of the missing poem? I mean apart from continuing the search."

"Well, I suppose I could just choose a poem, more or less at random, and make use of it. Maybe I will eventually get comfortable with it."

"Right, let's pretend you have learned the words of a poem and you are driving along a main road. Just try to imagine the situation for moment."

"Yes, I'm happy with that. As a matter of fact I have a new car so already I feel more confident but I suppose you're going to hit me with another problem. In my mind I'm beginning to think about my protective poem."

"In that case you are doing well, you've anticipated what might happen and you are already preparing your defenses. How do you feel?"

"I feel much better than I would have done a few days ago."

"Good. Now let's take another scenario. Pretend you are in a rowing boat out on a lake in the park."

"Right. I've got that. It's a cloudy day and I am the only one out in a boat today."

"I want you to imagine that the boat springs a leak and your feet are getting wet. What goes through your mind?"

"It's a bit more frightening than the car because I am not used to boats and I can't swim, but I suppose I should start rowing ashore before the boat sinks. Once I've made the decision to make for the shore I feel a bit safer and start to think about taking my mind off of the danger. Time for some distractive conversation I suppose."

How are you doing with the imaginary protective poem?"

"Well, to tell you the truth, I'm not sure that I am using an imaginary poem for my protection. I am making up something as I go along. I feel perfectly content because I am doing something creative. I am writing poetry in my head. Wow, that's a fantastic way to generate a conversation when there's no-one around! I can create the other side of the conversation and then stand back and admire my own work. I can feel myself feeling proud of myself."

At this point the client is relaxed and smiling. It is time to end the session and the process. The client is using a conscious thought process to successfully cope with the future by adopting a technique developed for his/her own benefit. Clients who do this own the solution and have confidence in its effectiveness. The future begins to look bright for them.

"Congratulations, you seem to have come to understand yourself and your reaction to this sort of incident. What is even more important and valuable is the fact that you have found a unique way of dealing with your reaction and overcoming the consequences. If you like, we can run through a few more imaginary scenarios and see how you cope with them. On the other hand, we can take your obvious confidence as a signal that tells us our work together is done."

"Thank you so much for your help. I really don't think I need to have any more of this artificial practice. I think you've helped me to become a poet who's not afraid of anything anymore.

My words can now allay my fears,
And they can drive away my tears,
I never need to feel alone
Even if I am on my own."

"Well done. That's a lovely and useful verse. It seems like you've really made it to the end of the process. If you agree, I should like to call this the end of today's session and the end of the counseling program. I wish you all the best for the future."

The client now has confidence in self and the new solution. In this case he/she seems to have already begun to implement the solution in anticipation of difficulties as a proactive defense mechanism rather than a reactive coping strategy. That is, of course, an ideal outcome.

Sample Reinforce Questions

In this session we need to find out how the client feels about the future and reinforce the benefits of the Cognitive Analysis. It is also appropriate to make constructive suggestions or recommendations that may prove useful in any similar emergency situations in the future. The typical questions might be:

- "How do you feel now?"
- "How would you solve the problem now?"
- "What will you do next time?"

Reinforce Session Goals

The counselor is seeking to bring out recommendations and reinforcement of new feelings and more appropriate solutions. This should then lead on to rehearsal of the new behavior pattern. One can construct imaginary situations and mentally explore the client's considered reactions. These considered reactions should be based on the discoveries and realizations developed in the previous two sessions.

The Reinforce session is the final preparation for the client to be able to handle things on his/her own without recourse to the previous ineffective behavior pattern. The client should begin to feel secure about the future.

The primary objective is to stabilize the benefits the client has developed, in order to ensure that the client is now able to face the future confidently. The new, better behavior pattern has to be practiced and developed to the point where it can be relied upon to stand the client in good stead under all circumstances. This final session is where we need to reinforce the new feelings and solutions and make useful practical recommendations that will enable the client to venture forth with the certain knowledge that he or she can cope with a similar event, or situation, should it ever crop up.

A very useful additional tool for a client at this stage is the *Dark Serpent Technique*, in which we get them to imagine various problems and get into the habit of solving them in a number of different ways (as detailed in Chapter 9.)

4 Guidelines for the Counselor

The ideal counselor brings a *neutral attitude* to the counseling session. The counselor works to and with the client's standards and attitudes, not his/her own. There should be no hint of antagonism, fear, anger or any other emotion, no implied judgment or criticism. This impartial acceptance of the client's own worldview makes the client feel safe and free to discuss his or her innermost feelings. The moment this sense of security is compromised, the client will withdraw from the counselor and the session. The degree of withdrawal will depend upon the client's emotional state, general tolerance threshold and the amount of attitude revealed by the counselor. If this should happen, it is possible to patch up the counselor/client relationship. (See Session Recovery on p. 71)

However, it is best to have all aspects of the session run smoothly, and this can be achieved by sticking to the proposed Code for Counselors as shown in Fig. 4-1 on p. 36.

Solving (confronting and handling) one small problem restores a person's ability to solve other, bigger problems. Solving remote or invented problems will also help to restore the problem solving ability. Looking at problems that are even bigger than the one being handled will improve a client's attitude toward problem solving, thus enhancing their ability to confront and deal with problems in general.

DO NOT	EVALUATE (i.e. do not give your opinion) INTERRUPT JUDGE REACT (i.e., Do not become emotional) INTERPRET (i.e. Do not rephrase)
DO	ACKNOWLEDGE (each answer/statement of the client) ACCEPT as "TRUE" the client's worldview RETAIN CONTROL GIVE POSITIVE REPLIES (as few as needed)

Fig. 4-1: Code for Counselors

(See both Chapter 8 and the Glossary for a full definition of the above terms)

The End Point

Each session should last up to about an hour. The end point of a session should be dependent upon the client's frame of mind, not the clock. If the client agrees he or she has made progress and has positive indicators the session can, and should, be brought to a close.

Positive indicators are a combination of the following:

a) A smile,

b) A statement of feeling good and not being bothered by the incident, indicating a degree of relief,

c) A willingness to go out and face the world.

The importance of this concept of a definite *end point* to a session or a process cannot be overstressed. If the end point is not reached, the client is left brooding over the incident which has been restimulated, yet no relief has been experienced. In this situation, client may develop the view that this Restabilization is not working and probably will not work; furthermore they will feel their increased unhappiness is due to the counselor who offered to help. The end result of this thought process might be:

> *"Help is a Trap—people only offer to help so they can do you harm."'*

If, on the other hand, you go past the end point without acknowledging it and ending the session, a similarly unsatisfactory result is obtained. Overrunning the session or action invalidates a client's progress. People who have been overrun may feel as though the original hurt may be gone, but the dim memory of an earlier similar occasion has been restimulated. As a result, they feel unhappy about something, but they are not sure what. Consequently, they may withdraw from further communication with the counselor who caused this upset. The emotion of an earlier hurt is now there, in restimulation, and a further sense of loss has been added to make it even worse.

These two basic errors, incomplete and overrun sessions, frequently cause upsets and traumas in counseling. When help only leads them on to further pain, an overwhelmed client can feel as if the world is collapsing around them.

Diagnosis

After a crisis, any change to a person's normal behavior pattern must be regarded as an indication of a potential problem that needs to be addressed. The specific symptoms of a person who would benefit from Restabilization might include:

- Restlessness or difficulties with sleeping.

- Increased lethargy or tiredness where there is no apparent cause such as late nights or poor sleep.

- Feeling more tense than usual, or a sense of anticipation or excitement that has no obvious justification (also called hyper-arousal). May include exaggerated startle reactions;

- A higher accident or error rate than normal. (Some of their attention is fixed on another event at another time or place.)

- Feeling disorganized or unable to concentrate, they may also feel slightly disoriented or out of place and perhaps unsure of themselves.

- Withdrawing either physically or mentally from the scene of the event (also called *avoidance* in the literature). Immune system may be more susceptible.

According to the US National Center for PTSD, the following other symptoms may appear as well:

- Reliving the event (also called re-experiencing symptoms or "flashbacks").

- Feeling numb and unable to express any feelings, loss of interest in relationships or normal activities.

- Forgetting about parts of the traumatic event or not being able to talk about them.

They may experience or exhibit any one or more of these symptoms to a greater or lesser degree in more or less any combination and perhaps only occasionally, when something restimulates their subconscious reaction to the crisis.

| 5 | # The Personal View of Crisis | |

Most crises reflect a failure of personal logic: "What has always worked now does not work." Over the years we have learned to cope by solving the various problems life has thrown at us. This certainty of our own ability to cope is what enables us to face upheaval with some degree of confidence. Once that confidence is severely shaken, we have a personal crisis on our hands. Occasionally, there are lasting consequences such as death of a loved one or disability as well.

The sequence of rationalization taking place in the subconscious part of the mind goes something like this:

- System failure.
- Confusion.
- Fear of the future and what it may hold.
- Ineffective behavior.
- Panic.
- Feeling that life is meaningless.
- Want to return to "as before".

The subconscious reasoning goes something like this:

1) I cannot solve this set of problems, my survival system has failed me, it is no longer dependable.

2) I am afraid of the future because it is unknown and therefore possibly full of insoluble problems.

3) I am unable to think things through properly (my behavior is ineffective or maladaptive).

4) Observing my own strange behavior, I begin to panic and behave even more erratically.

5) My life no longer has any meaning or purpose; I can't cope with this very bleak prospect.

6) I just want to return to the "as before" situation where life was worthwhile.

In the attempt to return to the "as before", the distressed mind may well seek refuge in the most comfortable of all the possible "as before" scenarios. The end result could well be a return to childhood or even babyhood, when life was safe and comfortable. This leads to what we see and recognize as childish behavior. Naturally, people in some situations are behaving like children. For all intents and purposes they are children, driven back in time by a failure to cope with a current situation. For others, the days of childhood were not the most comfortable ones, and the mind might find some other more suitable period to withdraw into. This may or may not be easy to recognize or detect.

What seems to occur subconsciously to the victim of multiple traumatic events over the course of years can also be called the *descending slope*. The further down the slope we go, the more likely it is that we will continue on down (see Fig. 5-1). The downward progress is self-perpetuating and self-sustaining. The steps get steeper and more slippery as we descend. This is why we must get the client facing and reaching upward as soon as possible.

SESSION MODELS

The counselor should work each session to a pattern, or model, which includes all the essential elements—in the right order. Notes should be taken to ensure continuity between sessions—but note-taking should not be allowed to divert the counselor's attention away from the client.

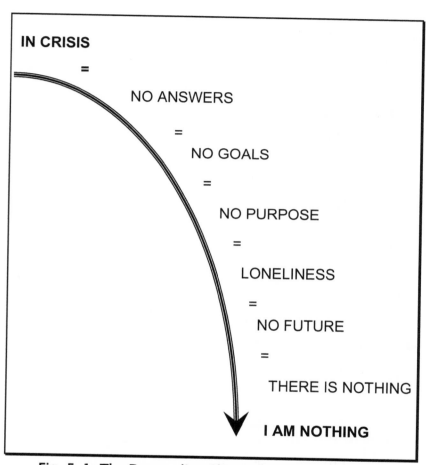

Fig. 5-1: The Descending Slope of Repeated Trauma

One-on-One Session Model

These models are given to ensure that the counselor understands exactly what is and what is not relevant to the Restabilization process. The irrelevancies are more than a mere waste of time—they actually detract from the usefulness of the process!

1	**Does the client feel safe, and is willing to talk?** E.g., "Is this room OK for us to talk in?"
2	**Formally start the session** E.g., "We are now starting the session—anything you say will be held in absolute confidence."
3	**Establish Progress to Date** E.g., "In our last session we got to ____ and now we shall move on to _____." (In the first session, step 3 is omitted.)
4	**Define the Session Purpose** E.g. "Today we are going to look at ____."
5	**Perform the appropriate Session Actions**.
6	**Agree Session Progress** E.g., "We have looked at _____ and you have found _____." (Obtain client's agreement and positive indicators.)
7	**Establish the next Session** E.g. "Our next session will be back here on ____. Thank you for talking to me today."
8	**Formally end the session.** E.g., "That's it. End of the session."

Fig. 5-2: The One-on-One Session Model

Normal conversation can now take place and normal social conventions apply once more.

Group Session Model

In crisis the problem is, or at least appears to be:

1) Information is missing, leading to a sense of mystery.

2) There is not enough support available.

3) The alternatives appear to be hidden, i.e., the client is unaware of what might solve the problem more effectively.

So, the counselor or facilitator needs to:

1) Give and get more information.

2) Offer and give more support, as appropriate.

3) Make constructive suggestions about where and how alternatives might be found.

This type of approach often works better in a group where the counselor has the opportunity to speak generally, while giving information to the individual. (N.B. Although the group approach is appropriate and effective in this type of work, it may be ineffective in other counseling situations.)

The counselor and a co-worker, together with the client, can be set up to function as a group. The counselor can then give information to the co-worker for the benefit of the client. E.g. "Making notes always helps me to remember things," as an aside, provides data to the client who overhears the remark rather than receives instruction. Because this is a discovery by the client, rather than instruction from the counselor, it is more meaningful, and it is helping to repair the client's problem solving capability.

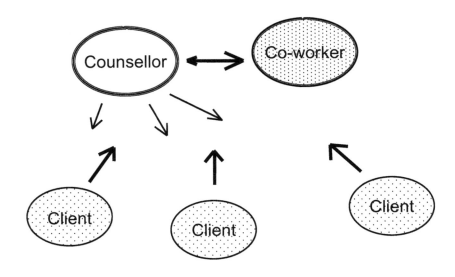

Fig. 5-3: Group session model with clients "overhearing"

Another advantage of the group approach is the self-sustaining quality of a group. It is possible to encourage the group to meet on a regular basis to share their views, problems and solutions. The group might become a strong self-supporting unit, made up of people who share a common bond and are developing (or re-developing) a sense of purpose for themselves.

Working with Groups

Invasion of Privacy

A large supermarket was located alongside the railway tracks which ran into a main line terminus. One morning, there was a train wreck immediately opposite their premises and the supermarket's car park was occupied by the emergency services as the base for the rescue work and the whole area was cordoned off. Very soon the approach road was full of TV cameras. Members of the supermarket staff were forced to evacuate and were unable to return to work for several days.

Group restabilization was offered and a large proportion of the work force elected to take part. During the first session, everybody was surprised to find that they shared a common reaction to the incident. The majority of them felt as though they had been invaded.

Typical expressions were "I felt it was an invasion of our privacy;" "We were being crowded out of our own space;" "They made the place feel dark and oppressive;" "I felt uncomfortable with all these strange people around."

The essence of these comments was captured on a flipchart, which we then tried to reduce to a common reaction or theme. Everyone agreed there had been an overwhelming sense of an "invasion of privacy" which then led to a sense of guilt as they began to realize it had been the scene of an enormous tragedy. People had lost their lives. Feelings had become muddled.

During the second session, we were able to plot what they called a "reaction line". It appeared that as events began to unfold, their emotions changed in accordance with the information available to them. The initial "invaded space" reaction was perfectly valid when the emergency services arrived unannounced. In fact, it was seen as a clear indication of how attached they all were to their place of work and their colleagues. It could be interpreted as a symptom of good team spirit and a sense of belonging.

Once they realized their "reaction line" was, in fact, a reflection of their state of knowledge, they were able to reconcile their feelings as being appropriate at that moment in time. We'll describe the reaction line in detail at the end of this chapter.

During the third session, everybody agreed that they should make a point of exchanging reactions whenever any thing unusual occurred in the future. In this way they felt they would all be able to share in developing, and sharing, an appropriate reaction. Somebody suggested: "Ten heads are better than one, and ten shoulders to cry on could be a great comfort. We are lucky to have each other."

Very few people turned up for the fourth session. When questioned later, they said they didn't feel the need for a special meeting to help each other face the future because they were doing that all the time anyway. As one of them said, "All's well that ends well."

The Smell of Fire

In 1987, the King's Cross fire[3] affected thousands of commuters. There was a major fire in an underground station beneath a mainline terminus. For weeks, thousands of passengers had to find alternative routes to work while the station was being rendered safe and refurbished. One company offered restabilization to employees who had been inconvenienced or affected by the fire and the subsequent travel problems.

There were two principal reactions to the event. "Fear of being trapped underground" and "fear of being burned alive." Despite reassurances from the public authorities, a core group felt they would never be safe traveling though King's Cross again. Even though the place had been thoroughly overhauled, the cause of the incident identified and eradicated, there was a permanent stigma in the minds of these people. One person suggested he could smell smoke every time someone mentioned the name of the place. The media had reported many instances of people maintaining they could smell smoke when traveling through or near to the scene of the tragic fire.

Restabilization did not appear to be able to reassure these victims about the physical safety of this traumatic location. They seemed to have lost trust in the system but they nevertheless felt it was worth meeting

---

3 See http://en.wikipedia.org/wiki/King's_Cross_fire

regularly to talk things through with each other. One person said: "I find it easy to talk about my concerns with these guys because they really do understand what I mean." Over the next six months or so the group got smaller and smaller. It seems that one by one they were able to confront their fears and suspicions and were going back to traveling to work on the underground. They may not have been cured but they had managed to learn to cope.

Suicide Inferno

This incident occurred in a small overseas branch of a Middle-Eastern bank. A man had emptied a petrol can and set fire to himself in the customer area. Immediately the fire alarm had gone off, everything shut down and the place was plunged in darkness, except for the burning carpet and the flaming body. Shortly afterward, the bank had relocated its key operations to a standby recovery site. It was there that we offered our services to the staff. Most of them didn't feel they needed help at that stage; perhaps it was too early or maybe they were unaffected because it was all over so quickly. These conclusions ran counter to our intuition, but you cannot help someone who denies assistance.

However, the two young lady cashiers did want to try working things through as a small group. Neither of them wanted to be alone, they were literally clinging on to each other for comfort. They could not bear to be parted.

During the first session, they both gave a clear picture of just what had happened. Everything seemed to have occurred in slow motion for both of them. They agreed about how they had sat and watched this man empty the gasoline can and slowly take a lighter out of his pocket. Then the flames spread slowly until suddenly all the lights went out and the fire alarm sounded. Finally the man ran out of the door, still ablaze from head to toe, and they found themselves clinging to each other in total darkness. One of them called out: "Come back, we can't see."

Apparently they had both felt a sense of loss when the man ran away, taking their only source of light with him. They also shared the almost instant regret of putting their fear of the dark before feeling sorry for the man who was obviously in agony. When they heard he was still live although badly burned, they felt slightly better about it but they were still hung up with their guilt. One interesting realization was about the high degree of affinity which had developed between them in the time they had worked together. Their bonding was so strong they found themselves thinking the same thoughts at the same time.

Gradually they both learned to come to terms with what was after all a perfectly natural reaction to such an unusual, almost surreal, situation. On this occasion, the four stages of Restabilization were explored the following day. The sessions were run sequentially with short breaks in between. As they gained a better understanding of how and why they had reacted and began to figure out some alternative solutions, their initial nervousness began to wane and gradually they were able to let go of each other's hands. By the end of the afternoon they were able to stand well apart and mix with the rest of their colleagues.

A few days later, everybody returned to their normal place and routine of work. There were no further calls upon our services.

Phoenix Society

A merger between two firms led to a need for some downsizing and cutbacks, which were not handled very fairly or sympathetically. The consultancy division bore the brunt of these dealings and brought themselves together to deal with both the employment and the emotional problems which faced them. Because of the nature of their work, several of the participants were familiar with the basic premise of Restabilization and decided to follow its procedure for themselves.

The upshot of their discussions was the launch of an informal self-help group, which they called the Phoenix Society. Membership was confined to those who had been involved in the saga of the job losses, cutbacks and legal but vicious treatment. Each member pledged to find work for themselves and their fellow Phoenicians wherever possible. Most of them decided to set themselves up as independent practitioners, while others hoped to find full time employment. The group as a whole pledged to provide temporary financial support to any member who got into difficulty as a result of being made redundant ("fired").

Fortunately, the financial support measure was never called upon. Everyone found gainful employment within a relatively short period of time and seven years later they are still in touch with each other and working together on a regular basis. It is generally felt among the group that the positive attitude the Phoenix Society helped them to adopt was a key element in their subsequent success.

Reaction Line Plotting

Throughout the whole process of restabilization we are attempting to help the client deal with their current reaction to a specific event or set of circumstances. During the process their view of the incident, and therefore their reaction to it, will evolve. This is how they manage to discharge their emotions in relation to the incident and develop a more practical coping strategy to deal with similar events in the future. The changes may occur in small steps heading in the right direction or they may be the result of a sudden insight or cognition which results in a radical alteration of their thinking.

When working with an individual client it seems perfectly normal for their current view and reaction to be a private picture held within their own mind's eye. However, when working with a group it is more important for everyone, clients and counselor included, to have a common understanding of the current picture, or pictures, which people have of the incident. One particular group went so far as to suggest making a visual record of the reactions which people within the group were experiencing. The original idea was simply to obtain agreement about the range of emotions which were in play at that particular time. We captured a few cryptic phrases which encapsulated the various individual views. In fact many people shared similar views. One could say that a common emotional model of the event was developing, although that was not our intention.

In a later session, when we tried to capture the improved picture it became obvious that something was happening. Everybody was developing a more pragmatic and less emotive attitude to the disturbances caused by the recent emergency. This became the basis of what we came to call the 'reaction line'. As we continued with the process we were able to show how things had improved through open communication and rational thinking. Our reaction line was, in effect, a progress chart which helped to reinforce the progress which was being made, boosting their confidence in their own ability to conquer their fears and deal with the future in a more constructive manner.

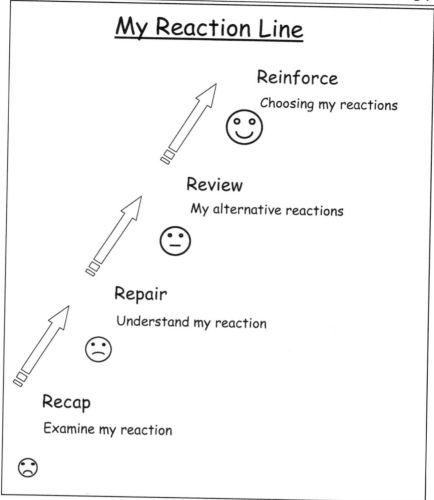

My Reaction Line

Reinforce

Choosing my reactions

Review

My alternative reactions

Repair

Understand my reaction

Recap

Examine my reaction

Fig. 5-4: Reaction Line Diagram

By using different colored marker pens on a flip chart we were able to distinguish between the moods and achievements of the four stages of restabilization. In effect, this is a time line indicating the improvements attained during each of those stages. Time lines are usually drawn either as horizontal lines with markers indicating particular milestones or as a graph plotting time against a specific parameter such as value, percentage growth or some other measurable characteristic. Personally, I prefer to portray the reaction line as a growth path starting at the bottom, moving forwards and upwards towards a specific goal. This gives a visual impression of the scope and extent of the coming journey. There are only four clear steps and the destination is diagonally opposite the starting point. Whilst there is a hint of an uphill struggle there is also the implication of a logical approach with a positive outcome.

Since discovering the reaction line, I have come to appreciate its value and sometimes use it in a one-on-one case as an educational tool to help the client understand how the process is supposed to work. As the case progresses we can work together at filling in the details of their changing reactions. This seems to help to reinforce the benefits obtained during each of the sessions. Progress can be indicated by the use of little cartoon faces. These could be drawn on the flipchart at the appropriate time or added in the form of small Post-It notes. Another possibility would be to have them pre-drawn and hidden by Post-It notes; ready to be revealed at the end of each session. Obviously, one has to exercise a certain amount of discretion when thinking about adding what might be seen as a humorous touch. Some clients seem to welcome the opportunity to have a little smile, whilst others might consider it inappropriate in connection with such a serious process as their recovery from the impact of a tragedy.

If you are ever in doubt about the use of humor in such a situation it is best to refrain. Insensitive humor can do a lot of damage to any relationship, especially where one of the participants is already feeling the strain of unwelcome feelings.

The reaction line can be seen as the tracking of a person's attitudes towards a particular type of situation in the light of reviewing their considerations and processing relevant information about themselves in relation to the environment and its events. With the help of effective counseling this reaction line can be expected to show an upward trend towards more comfortable behavior. Without such help, the reaction line is more likely to show a downward trend towards less comfortable behavior.

A Typical Reaction Line

In this incident the client had been injured in an accident which occurred whilst working with unfamiliar equipment.

The Recap session revealed:

- Pain and confusion which was soon replaced by a sense of loss (loss of dignity and self-confidence) causing withdrawal from the scene.

The Review session revealed:

- A need to apportion blame leading to blaming both self and others for allowing, or causing, this to happen.

The Repair session revealed:

- The need to allocate and accept responsibility for the environment and one's actions within it.

The Reinforce session revealed:

- A laughingly declared intention to 'read the f—ing instructions' and a resolve to adopt a rather more cautious approach when dealing with anything unfamiliar.

6 Opportunity Meetings

This first meeting should be held as soon as possible after the crisis event. There are two possible scenarios here:

1) Many people were exposed to the crisis.

2) A small number of individuals were exposed.

In the first instance, the survivors should be called to an open opportunity meeting where the incident is freely described and Restabilization is offered to those who feel they might benefit. In the second case, a more intimate meeting is preferable, in which the incident is briefly covered and the opportunity for Restabilization is described. The message is the same; only the size of the audience is different.

Open Opportunity Meeting

In a business environment, senior management (which might be interpreted as "those responsible" or 'the organizers') should make it clear to the invited audience that there has been a disastrous event and things are now under control. The audience should be told how this event will affect them and their jobs. They should also be told what management's official stance will be to the outside world.

After this recognition of the root cause of any potential staff problems, the audience should be told about the counseling program on offer to them. The possible need for Restabilization should be made clear and the symptoms described. Ideally, the counselor should be introduced and allowed to reassure everyone that the counselors' code of conduct will ensure everything is said and done in the very strictest confidence. The room(s) where the counseling will take place should also be made known. People will be looking to be counseled in what they consider to be a safe, comfortable environment. Their manager's own office or the worksite's canteen (cafeteria) may not qualify as safe and/or comfortable.

In the absence of a space they recognize as safe, they will not consider taking the first step of approaching the counselor or, more accurately, visiting the counselor's territory, which needs to be attractive to them. The principal attractions they will be seeking are peace and quiet combined with privacy and some degree of comfort. Ideally, the approach route should be discreet, away from the public gaze. The room should be warm and plainly but pleasantly furnished.

A Typical Management Statement

At the Open Opportunity Meeting, management should make a public statement along the following lines:

> "After any severely traumatic event, people can have a wide variety of reactions and may therefore benefit from some form of counseling, designed to help them understand and deal with those reactions. Accordingly we are making a (team of) counselor(s) available to all of you. Counseling will take place during normal office hours in the board room, which is to be dedicated to this purpose for the next six weeks. Board meetings will be held off-site, meanwhile."

> "We should all speak with a counselor if we notice any signs of stress or changes in our normal behavior pattern. The specific symptoms might include:

Increased lethargy or tiredness, tension, excitement, a higher accident or error rate, anger or frustration. Feeling disorganized, disoriented or withdrawn."

"A person may experience any one, or more, of these symptoms to a greater or lesser degree."

Anyone who was linked to the place, the time, the people or the property of the Trigger Event, will have been exposed to its after-effects. It should be made perfectly clear to all those who were exposed that it is completely normal for anyone to be thrown off balance by such a traumatic event.

There should be no barriers, real or imagined, that might discourage anyone from taking part in the program. It should be free in every sense of the word.

An Opportunity Meeting

The corporate headquarters of a successful communications company was a tall office block, which provided comfortable office space for several hundred people. The canteen was on the top floor overlooking the gardens at the rear of the building. One summer lunchtime, a young man fell to his death from the balcony outside the canteen. The police closed the canteen and the garden while they carried out their investigations. Eventually the young man's body was taken away. During this period, rumors and gossip began to circulate and many members of staff were clearly disturbed by what had happened.

All scheduled meetings were cancelled until further notice and the directors took it upon themselves to address everyone through a series of emergency meetings. They spent a few minutes in the board room agreeing their strategy before speaking to the various groups of people who were assembled in meeting rooms throughout the building. These meetings were held more or less simultaneously so everyone got the same message at the same time.

The directors worked in pairs and were accompanied by some of the senior managers. This enabled them to be seen to be supporting each other rather than toughing it our on their own. A typical meeting went something like this:

> "Good afternoon ladies and gentlemen, Tony and I have just come from an emergency board meeting where we heard about the unfortunate demise of a valued member of staff this lunch time. The police are currently conducting a preliminary investigation into the cause of the fall and we are expecting the Health and Safety Executive to be carrying a rather more thorough investigation over the next couple of days.

> At the moment, the authorities are keeping an open mind about the cause and will want to interview anyone who was a witness to the incident. They may also wish to speak to people who worked closely with the deceased.

> We, the directors and managers, feel the burden of responsibility lies firmly on our shoulders. We are also deeply upset and find it difficult to concentrate upon the business at hand while this cloud of doubt and sorrow hangs over all of us.

> Our emotional response is perfectly normal; indeed we'd be rather peculiar people if the death of a friend and colleague didn't affect us. Therefore we are arranging for a team of counselors to visit us tomorrow and explain how they can help us to understand what happened and our reactions to it. They will then be available to offer either individual or group support for all members of staff who feel they might be able to benefit from the counseling process.

We'd advise everyone to seriously consider attending these counseling sessions even if you don't feel you have any symptoms that need to be dealt with. Your presence as a member of the group may help others to come to terms with what happened. In any case, you should attend the first meeting tomorrow morning. The counselors will explain to you how their restabilization technique works and describe the symptoms you might be experiencing. Of course nobody is forced to attend, we each have our own way of dealing with grief and for some of you it might be a very private affair. In that case you may attend private, anonymous counseling sessions, which will be available in the interview rooms on the ground floor over the next few weeks.

For the time being, please feel free to remain on the premises and try to do some work or just sit and chat with your friends and colleagues. Take the rest of the day off if you prefer. The choice is yours, we are not expecting a full day's work from anyone for the next few days. The first of the counselors' meetings will be held here, starting at about ten o'clock tomorrow morning."

As a matter of politeness, the audience were invited to ask questions about the counseling program although it was pointed out that there was no information available about the incident. However, the directors did promise to keep everyone informed of any developments or news about their dead colleague.

Most of the staff turned up for the first meeting with the counselors and about 20% followed this up with group or individual counseling. The clients comprised those who knew the victim, witnessed the incident or worked in the same department. Counselors were freely available for the next four weeks although they had very few attendees after the first week of fairly intense work.

There was no evidence of abnormal absenteeism after the first few days and the turnover of staff remained at the normal level in the months to come.

| 7 | Essential Counseling Skills |  |

A counselor must have a thorough understanding of how to, and how not to, communicate before being effective at handling other people's problems. This is especially so if they don't share any common ground on which to build a relationship. Next, we look at communication: how to improve it and how to control it. These skills are of paramount importance to the successful counselor. Effective counseling is virtually impossible without these skills.

Interpersonal Skills – Communication

We normally communicate with each other in order to gain or transfer understanding. An alternative reason for communicating is pure amusement. While amusement is not a bad thing, in business it is often helpful if we manage to achieve the first objective. In order to gain an understanding of how to communicate, we should first review the basic mechanics of communication and *communion.*

As all of our relationships with others depend on communication and communion. What we are looking at here is useful to all of us in everything we do, or want to do, or want to have done to us, or for us.

Communion (Gerbode, 1995) has three interdependent components: communication, comprehension, and affection (see Fig. 7-1 on following page).

If we increase any one of these three components, then we will increase the degree of communion and improve the other two components at the same time.

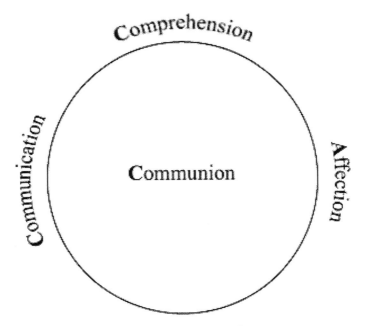

Fig. 7-1: The Components of Communion

For example: I don't understand children because I have no experience of them as an adult. Unknown or misunderstood areas of life lead to disbelief and disinterest (don't really want to know). Then I actually meet a child and develop rapport. Suddenly my disinterest changes; I now comprehend children better because I have communicated with one. As a result, my affection has risen both for that child and possibly for children in general. Either I have developed sympathy for them or dispelled my fear of the unknown. Now I definitely have some communion with children. I will communicate with them further and perhaps read about them and gradually develop a deeper understanding of them. All of this understanding takes place in the context of my previous education, experience and perception of the world in which I live.

I assert that dullness or stupidity about any given subject is most often the result of a misunderstanding: I leave my car unlocked because I don't really understand why I should lock it. If, by experience or explanation, I come to realize that there are a number of criminals in the neighborhood who might steal my car, I might reconsider my attitude toward locking it. However, what is really going to change my mind is an understanding of the many reasons why someone might attempt to open my car. These reasons would include:

> To steal and sell, to steal and use, to joyride, to remove and sell the radio, to steal and sell my personal things, to steal and use my cassettes, to enjoy causing damage etc., etc.

It is important that you and your audience know the meanings of all the words and idioms you use. This means you should carefully avoid the use of jargon, explain the meaning of any technical terms, and always try to use a style of language familiar to the listener.

The Communication Cycle

Communication is the interchange of concepts across space, and has to be bi-directional to be complete, even if one of the directions is only an assumption or a "virtual" response.

The full cycle of communication is only complete when an acknowledgement has been received by the originator. First, the originator gets an idea or concept which he or she causes to travel across a distance to the receiver, who receives the effect in the form of a concept. In order to complete the cycle, the receiver causes the concept of an acknowledgement to travel back to the originator to confirm that the original message arrived, and the cycle is therefore complete. As nothing is left outstanding, further communication can continue easily and smoothly.

For example I might say "Hello" to a stranger and receive a smile, which indicates to me that my "Hello" arrived, was heard and understood. I would then feel we were in communication, and I have the attention of the stranger. I might then proceed to offer my help with a question like "Can I help you?" If I were to get the response of "NO", I would take that as a refusal of my willingness to help, which would disappoint me and make me reluctant to continue any conversation with this stranger. It might also deter me from offering help to strangers in the future. If I get the response of "Thank you," I would feel that my offer had been validated and accepted. The combination of "No, but thank you anyway" would give me the impression that my offer was recognized and validated, although help was not actually required. Both parties would feel satisfied.

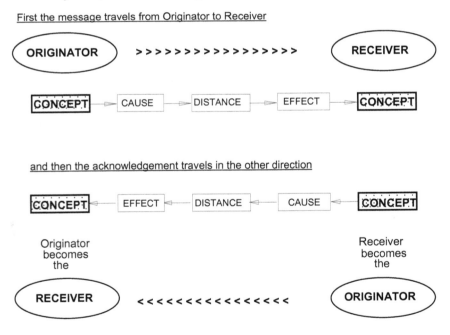

Fig. 7-2: The Communication Cycle

Control—or the Cycle of Action

Control consists of the ability to begin, modify and end any action. E.g., in order to prove I can drive a manual car, I must be able to get it to move (begin) by using the gears and clutch more or less correctly. Good control implies doing it smoothly. Then I would have to steer it to avoid any obstacles and other road users (modify direction). At the same time, I would need to adjust the speed of the car according to the road conditions (modify speed) and also ensure the engine was not overloaded (modify gear). Finally, I would have to park the car safely before I passed my test (end).

The same cycle of action applies to communication or conversation. In order to control the communication, you must be able to demonstrate that you can begin, modify and end the communication at will. Otherwise, either someone else is in charge of the conversation, or no-one is in control.

Preparation

To be effective in controlling a conversation, you must:

a) Have the ability to control it;
b) Know what you are trying to achieve;
c) Know how to achieve your objective;
d) Know whether you achieved your objective.

Without some kind of structure or plan for this conversation, you will probably fail on all four counts. It is not necessary to have a complex plan, but there are some set patterns you can use to good effect almost all of the time.

These patterns have the effect of enabling you to focus on the data you want to get or the data you want to give.

Structured Conversation

In order to get the best from a conversation, you need to have a few bullet points prepared in advance (not necessarily on paper), and once you have achieved each mini-objective you can move smoothly onto the next. Finally, in order to be sure you achieved your objective(s), it is wise to recap and get agreement about what has been said. If you do not have agreement, then you can work out what the difference is and fix it before re-recapping and agreeing.

Often you will want to get information and give information in the same conversation. In that case, your plan needs to include when you go from one role to the other. It will also include some guidelines about what information you give, which may depend upon some of the answers you receive. While it is often essential for you to think on your feet, it is so much easier if you remove as many of the elements of chance as you can, in advance. A little forethought will help to manage and control a conversation with a lot less effort. Why struggle for success when you can prepare your own guarantee?

Conversation Control

To exercise control over a conversation, we have to be able to begin, modify, and end it. Each of these stages is worth practicing until you can do it smoothly and effortlessly.

Starting means ensuring that a useful conversation is going to take place, rather than simply going through an exchange of pleasantries. It is quite possible for two people to be making noises at each other for hours on end, without any communication actually taking place.

Changing, in this context, often means ending one communication cycle and starting another. You can complete a cycle by ensuring that both of you have exchanged data about the current concept, or by bridging over to another subject, or a different aspect, by posing another question or making another statement. We can agree about the completion of the current communication cycle if we use an acknowledgement such as

"Thanks for telling me," "I do see what you mean" etc. Without this agreement, the other party's attention will still be stuck on the previous concept.

Another aspect of change is the ability to "not-change" or to stay on the same concept. Often we can elicit more information from someone by getting them to continue in the same vein, but we do need to watch that they are still contributing, and steer them if necessary. Here we need to use the *partial acknowledgement,* which is more of a comma than a full stop. A partial acknowledgement would be something like "What happened after that?" "I begin to see what you mean," etc.

Stopping a conversation is perhaps the most difficult for many of us, but all good things must come to an end, otherwise they cease to be good things. Once you have achieved your planned objective(s) it is wise to disengage gently, and terminate the conversation. "It's been very interesting talking to you, I do hope it has been useful to you and I look forward to seeing you again soon."

To bring people firmly into the reality of where they are, it is a sound idea to make them fully aware of where they are, and why they are there. I also like to establish with them just exactly what role they are in for the period of the session.

This is how to get an audience properly established in the role of an audience. If they do not realize they are the audience, they will not be expecting to pay attention to what you are going to say.

1. Get them to look around the room and feel the solidness of the environment. Make them aware of everything about the place and get them to do some action: "Stand up, sit down, feel the chair, what color is the wallpaper?" etc.

2. Tell them what the conversation is going to be about and get them to confirm that they want to hear

about that subject from you. "Today I'm going to tell you all about bicycles, is that OK with you?"

3. Get them to express, or consider, just what role they are playing today. John Doe is a complex creature who regularly wears a number of *identities*. At various times he may be:

A father	A husband	A driver	A student
A golfer	A manager	A teacher	A worker

Ask him to introduce himself, so he knows which identity he should be occupying. Demonstrate how it is done: "My name is Paul Newman, a famous movie star. I am here today to teach you how to tell stories. Now you tell me who you are, and why you are here."

4. Where possible, introduce some object or movement into the situation. If the subject is cycling—show them a bicycle, or a film of a bicycle, preferably in motion. Handouts are very useful to add mass and movement; you can get them to fill in their name, to identify their material.

Communication Exercises (CEs)

Before you set out to counsel a client, especially one with emotional problems, you must develop some degree of self-control. If you are unable to comfortably face your listeners and their problems, you will never be able to influence or assist them. Firstly, you must get your own act together, only then can you think about helping others.

I have included a series of communication exercises[4], which you can do in order to acquire the ability to deal with people and handle communication. These drills need to be performed in sequence and each one should be completed before you move on to the next. Done properly, in ascending sequence, they form a steady gradient. You will not derive the maximum benefit by working on a shorter track, so please do them in order. You can also go around the loop more than once, to get the most out of these exercises.

Each exercise is done with a twin, or co-student, who sits in a chair facing you a couple of feet away. You should take turns to act as trainer and student, although the trainer remains the same for the duration of any *one* exercise until complete. The trainer watches for any reaction and calls out "Stop"; and then tells the student what he/she saw. E.g. "Stop, you smiled."

CE #1: Being Present. Just sit with your eyes closed in the presence of the trainer until you can do so without reacting.

CE #2: Confronting. Sit with your eyes open, looking at the trainer, and do so without reacting.

CE #3: Maintaining Confront. Sit with your eyes open (as in CE #2) and the trainer says things to get the student to react. Could include comments about their appearance, demeanor, attitude, or even non-sequitors.

CE #4: Delivery. Read a phrase from a book and "deliver" it to the trainer. The student is stopped if the message does not arrive fresh and clear. If the message does arrive OK, then the trainer says so.

CE #5: Acknowledgment. Now the trainer reads a line from the book and the student gives a good, clear

---

[4] This section is a highly-abridged description of Communication Exercises taught in the *Traumatic Incident Reduction (TIR) Workshop*. See www.TIRtraining.org for more details.

full acknowledgment: e.g. "Good," "OK," "Fine," "Alright". The trainer reads the same line until the acknowledgment arrives clearly from the student.

CE #6) Encouraging Communication. Give partial acknowledgements to the trainer, which may be something like "Uh huh" or "Mmm hmm..." A partial acknowledgment encourages a person to go on talking by giving him/her the feeling both that you have received the communication and that you are waiting to hear more.

CE #7) Getting Your Questions Answered. As student, ask a question. If the reply does not answer it, then acknowledge their reply, and then ask the question again. Two simple questions are used alternately such as "Is the world round?" and "Will it rain?"

CE #8) Concerns. The student gets a question answered, handles any questions or worries the trainer brings up and smoothly returns to the question. Here the student must recognize what is relevant and clarify it if necessary, at the same time making the trainer feel the conversation is being smoothly controlled and his or her, statements are being received.

Communication Lag

When someone's attention is not really with you, or in the room, it is interesting to notice the length of time it takes them to give an answer to a simple question. Try asking someone a simple question like "Is the sky blue?" and see how long it takes them to give an answer. It doesn't matter whether the answer is right or wrong so much as how long it takes them to give their answer. At least, this is true from the dispersed attention point of view. A correct answer to a question is a measure of the amount of knowledge being applied, whereas a delayed answer is more a measure of the amount of attention being applied. It is a question of the timeliness rather than the correctness of the answer.

Session Recovery

If the counselor has broken the code of conduct and caused the client to "retreat" from the session, the trustful relationship has to be restored before any further counseling can be attempted. The case will have stalled, and little or no further progress can be made until the client's trust and willingness has been reestablished. Under this stalled situation, some counselors do continue to chip away for hours, weeks or even years without making any real progress. This leads to them accepting therapy as a lengthy process, to the extent that they deny the possibility of a speedy recovery, because they "know" it is lengthy and difficult.

To repair the relationship, one has to determine exactly what caused the breakdown. It may not be an obvious major upset; it is more likely to be a relatively minor matter that has reduced the original degree of rapport. Rapport, built on intention, attention, and communion, is what allows two people, including a client and counselor, to receive each other's communications clearly. Without this bridge there will be no flow of rapport, no communication, and hence no progress.

At the very beginning of the session, the counselor should try to determine if the rapport has deteriorated, and if so, determine the underlying cause. Accurately spotting the cause and talking about it, if necessary, will re-establish the original client-counselor relationship.

"Has there been a breakdown, upset, or loss in our working relationship?"
1) If there has been a breakdown:
    a) You invite the client to tell you all about it.

b) You may need to help the client spot what aspect of the relationship has deteriorated with the following questions:

"Has there been a change of attitude?"

"Has there been some disagreement?"

"Has there been some misunderstanding?

2) If the client denies such an upset, you should try to establish whether something is being (or has been) suppressed:

"Has anything been hidden or denied?"

Get the client to talk about the upset with a view of identifying the exact cause. When the client discovers the cause, you must acknowledge the discovery. (Failure to recognize and/or acknowledge is a common cause of a loss of client/counselor rapport).

"Alright, that was the cause of the upset. How does that seem to you now?"

The client should now show positive indicators, i.e., a smile and a willingness to continue with the session. If not, there may well be a previous similar incident which has been restimulated by this upset. It might, in fact, be one of a whole sequence of such events and you need to ask the client to spot them. Once the sequence has been handled properly, the client will feel very much better, possibly more cheerful than he/she has been for a long time. A string of unhandled upsets can cause people to sit in the middle of a vague, nagging sadness about relationships with "everyone" for years. Resolving past upsets rehabilitates the freedom to communicate properly.

If the client has spotted the cause of the recent upset, but is still sad or agitated or is unenthusiastic about continuing the session, then you need to track down the chain of previous upsets. You can start off by asking the question:

"Has something similar happened before?"

Get the client to talk about the previous upset and continue looking for earlier, similar upsets until the client spots the original root cause. The sequence of upsets is held together, like the links of a chain, because each one is a reminder of the original disturbing event. Identifying the underlying similar events will release all the emotional charge that has accumulated as the sequence has grown over the years.

| 8 | A Code for Counselors | |

A counselor should stick rigidly to the following Code of Practice when in session with a client. Once the session is closed, the normal social and professional rules of conduct apply.

WHEN IN SESSION,

DO NOT	EVALUATE (i.e. do not give your opinion)
	INTERRUPT
	JUDGE
	REACT (i.e. Do not become emotional)
	INTERPRET (i.e. Do not rephrase)
DO	ACKNOWLEDGE (each answer/statement of the client)
	ACCEPT as 'TRUE' the client's worldview
	RETAIN CONTROL
	GIVE POSITIVE REPLIES (as few as needed)

Fig. 4–1: Code for Counselors (repeated)

Acceptance: Whatever the client says, believes or appears to believe has to be accepted as true for them because it is the client's view of reality we are dealing with here. The counselor's view of the truth has no value to the client and could be detrimental or at best irrelevant to the client's progress; therefore the counselor must always accept the client's statements without hesitation or reservation[5].

---

[5] See "Reality and the Person Centered Approach" by Frank A. Gerbode, M.D. in *AMI/TIRA Newsletter*, Vol. 2, No. 2 (April 2005)

Acknowledge: An acknowledgement is not an indication of approval or disapproval, but simply that the statement has been received. It makes the client feel recognized as a participant in the process and accepted as a real person.

A firm acknowledgement ("OK," "Good," "Alright") can be used to complete a line of conversation, whereas a weak acknowledgement ("umm…", "Oh?", "well…") may simply fail to be heard and understood.

Control: The counselor must retain control of the conversation in order to provide a useful structure for the client's work. The counselor starts and ends the session. The client should be seated comfortably but alert.

React: The counselor should never act out or display reactions to the situation and produce yet another restimulator for the client. Any noticeable reaction will take the client's attention away from their own problem and may cause further upsets.

During a session, neither party is interested in the counselor's feelings, because both of you are dedicating your attention toward the client's well-being and progress. Show no surprise, anger, fear or any other emotion. You must have a "'neutral attitude" in your approach. Stick to the very minimum input from you and the maximum output from the client.

Evaluate: The counselor must avoid making any remarks which the client may regard as information about their condition or their rate of progress. Evaluation by the counselor will deter the client from evolving their very own, personally developed viewpoint of themselves and their progress, which is what we should be trying to achieve.

Interpret: The counselor must refrain from developing or re-phrasing a client's statement for them. Doing so will probably change the meaning and may come across as patronizing. Avoid phrases like "That's because..." or "What you mean is..." or "What you are try-ing to say is..." In this process we are primarily concerned with the client's view of reality, *not* whether you have a better way of describing it. It does not help the client to know how clever you are.

Interrupt: During a Restabilization session, the client is in touch with a special area of his/her consciousness. Any interruption will affect the flow of that communication within the client's mind and hence cause disturbance. In most modern societies, it is con-sidered to be rude to interrupt another person, for a very good reason. It is the opposite of an acknowledge-ment and implies "Your thoughts are unimportant: you might as well not exist."

Judge: The counselor must not show signs of judg-ing guilt or innocence, good or bad, fast or slow progress. Making any such judgments is not part of the counselor's role. All judgments must be the client's own. To assume the role of judge implies you are supe-rior, therefore they are inferior. This will spoil the client's relationship with the counselor, impairing fur-ther progress.

Positive Replies: During the Restabilization proc-ess, especially in session, the counselor should be asking the questions and the client should be respond-ing. However, there may well be situations where the client does need to seek information. Always give help-ful, willing replies. Even when you do not have the right answer, give the impression this problem can and will be resolved. For example,

- "I don't know of a painter offhand, but we can look in the *Yellow Pages*."
- "I am not a medical person, but I can help you find the number of a doctor."
- " I'm sure we will be able to find out."

It is better to coax the client to solve problems for themselves whenever possible, but do not allow them to fall into the trap of failing to solve a problem through lack of information. They do need to experience success. Where necessary, coach the client toward success rather than creating a dependency by becoming their butler or mother figure who can always be relied on to come up with the answers.

9	The Dark Serpent Dilemma and Technique	

In this technique, we take a hypothetical look at the various ways in which a person can deal with an unexpected problem. In effect they can be reduced to variations on five basic strategies which we will explain:

1. Succumb
2. Retreat
3. Ignore
4. Evade
5. Attack

These five basic approaches can be illustrated by reference to the Dark Serpent Dilemma. Let us suppose you come across a dark serpent lying on your garden path, and you want to get back into the house.

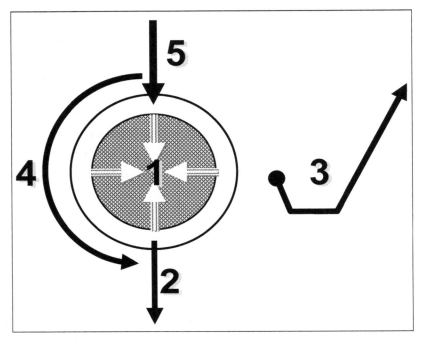

Fig. 9-1: The Dark Serpent Strategies

The basic strategies are shown here in diagrammatic form:

1. You may be rooted to the spot;
2. You might take fright and run away;
3. You can turn around and ignore the serpent, pretending it is not there;
4. You might consider taking a roundabout route trying to avoid it, hoping it will either leave you alone or fail to spot you.
5. You could attack the serpent, hoping to defeat it.

(At this point, choices such as bribery, flattery, and propitiation are not on offer.)

1. Attack

One approach to any kind of problem, including the Dark Serpent, is the direct frontal attack whereby we hope to solve the problem by recognizing it for what it is and using our mental and physical resources to overcome the difficulty in a more or less final confrontation. This approach often takes a degree of confidence or bravery, as well as some skill in implementing the solution. Inherent in attack is dealing with risks and consequences of failure.

With the Serpent, we could beat it to death with a stick—brutal but effective. We could threaten it with the stick, perhaps throwing in a few brave noises for good measure; braver but less certain. We could grab the snake by the tail and toss it over the garden wall; this would require considerable skill and bravado, although it may not be in the best interests of our neighbors. An expert might well recognize the Serpent as a harmless species or they might know how to drive it away by blowing smoke at it. This would, of course, require specialist knowledge and equipment.

These are the typical options within the attack strategy, which implies going straight ahead, and dealing with the problem in an appropriate manner. What is appropriate on one occasion may be reckless in many other situations.

2. Retreat

The opposite of the Attack strategy is to assume that the problem is not likely to be overcome, and simply run away from it. In the case of the Dark Serpent, this would mean running or walking away from the Serpent and this action could be justified by the common thought that it is better to run away and fight another day. That is the way in which one can accumulate a whole series of defeats without ever having fought a battle; the end result is a poor, insecure character who is afraid of everything and everyone. The Retreat strategy can take a number of forms and often involves some involved reasons, excuses or justifications for taking the easy way out or the soft option. As a default method of dealing with life's difficulties, it is not the route to success.

The "expert" might suggest that this particular species of Serpent is indestructible, highly venomous and has caused thousands of deaths. Another might claim they are allergic to snakes, but very few will admit that they run away from all problems as a matter of habit.

3. Evade

The third option is to try to avoid a direct conflict with the problem. In the case of the Dark Serpent, this might involve tiptoeing around the back of the bushes, going out of the back gate and going round the block to enter the house by the front door, or even climbing a tree and entering through a first floor window.

This route would be explained away as "I didn't want to disturb the snake, it looked so happy"—or "frightened", "pregnant", "asleep", or even "an endangered species" according to the expert.

In a real-life situation, the Evader would probably not want to cost the company all that money, or maybe there is no real need to invest time and effort on a problem that does not occur very often. The roundabout route is often quite complex and may be justified by virtue of the fact that it is "more interesting," "more scenic," "more educational" or whatever. The end result of adopting this as a default strategy is a devious character who pretends to himself as well as others. This deviousness may become a habit to the extent that such a person may no longer be capable of seeing things as they really are, let alone using simple straightforward solutions.

4. Ignore

The fourth option is to turn one's back on the problem and try to pretend it is not there. One would carry on gardening in the presence of the Dark Serpent, perhaps mistaking it for a hosepipe. Conceptually it is turning one's back and not recognizing the fact that there is a problem.

The classic way of dealing with a problem by ignoring it is to simply let all the difficulties mount up and take no action until forced to do so by outside circumstances. There are those who have difficulties with confronting their bills or accounts and consequently they get behind in all their payments until someone takes them to court—even then they pretend all is well. All is well, except for a slight oversight because they have been so busy (on holiday, away on business, off sick etc.) and they will offer to pay off all of their debts by the end of the week, even though there is nothing in their bank account. The true Evader does not even know there is no money there, for this person doesn't believe in reading bank statements because they are "so complex," "unreliable," "boring" or even "depressing."

5. Succumb

The final way of dealing with the Dark Serpent is to simply stay put and wait for it to bite, or possibly move away of its own accord. In any case there is nothing that the Succumber can do about it, except perhaps to cross their fingers. The habitual succumber is often highly superstitious, hoping their rabbit's foot, four leaf clover, clove of garlic or whatever will ward off the evil spirits.

Such people are at the mercy of their environment and will not be able to cope with walking under a ladder in the presence of a black cat, except when there are three magpies in sight or there is a G in the month.

Once one has learned how easy it is to succumb, (the trick is to be able to blame someone, or something, else e.g. "circumstances," "fate," "the weather," "the season," "the economy" etc.), it is tempting to succumb again and again and again. The end result is an apathetic approach to the challenges of life.

Taking Advantage of the Dark Serpent

The Dilemma of the Dark Serpent can be turned into a useful tool once we understand the underlying mechanism, which is a person's attempt to adopt a universal basis of solving all of life's problems. We can get the client to use the mechanism as a game-plan, to practice identifying imaginary problems and electing to solve them with the most appropriate strategy.

This type of exercise will enhance their ability to deal with life and its attendant problems, without exposing them unduly to real life and potentially stressful situations. It is an educational technique based on using the imagination within a safe environment rather than a learning exercise based on hard experience out in the field.

The Dark Serpent Technique (DST)

The Dark Serpent Technique is a way of enhancing the Restabilization process still further with a set of mental exercises that can help to develop a person's ability to cope with problems and situations.

It would be interesting to look back at the original Discoveries of Stress (see Preface) and align them with the Dark Serpent Strategies. You might even consider whether some of those Discoveries are a combination of more than one basic strategy.

DST – Step 1, Understanding the Strategies

To apply the Dark Serpent Technique to a client, one firstly explains the mechanism of the Dark Serpent Dilemma and the various possible Strategies . One then gets the client to look at examples of each strategy and get him or her to make these instances as realistic as possible by embroidering them with a great deal of detail.

DST – Step 2, Exploring the Strategies

The next stage of the process is to get the client to talk about specific dilemmas, again with as much detail as possible, and then explore each of the ways of handling that particular problem. The sequence in which you explore the five strategies is important. Start with the least active and work toward the most active strategy for any given situation. This regular approach helps to establish a pattern of thinking, which will help to ensure all possibilities are properly considered before a choice is made.

1. **SUCCUMB**
2. **RETREAT**
3. **IGNORE**
4. **EVADE**
5. **ATTACK**

One would ask questions like

- "Can you tell me about a problem you have handled?"

- "How did you handle it?"

- "Which strategy would you say that was?"

- "Which other strategies did you consider?"

    If the client has omitted one or more of the DST strategies from the reckoning, you should get him or her to consider the other alternatives, at least briefly.

- "Can you explain why you did not consider all of the other strategies?"

    For each strategy, have client try to think of as many variations as they can, exploring the reasons, justifications etc. that the problem solver would use or invent. You should also get them to look at the consequences of each solution, unless they include the consequences as a part of their rationale for choosing their strategy.

- "What were the consequences of the way you solved that problem?"

- "What might the consequences have been with some of the other strategies?"

Clients should be asked to review two or three past problems in this way before moving on to consider dealing with any possible future problems. After all, the past is relatively safe now we know what actually happened, whereas the future is always a bit uncertain.

DST – Step 3, Detecting a Pattern

Clients should be asked to consider whether or not there is a pattern to their problem solving. Are they inclined to automatically go for the same type of solution? It is worth explaining to them that there are two distinct versions of the Succumb Strategy: the Overt Succumb and the Covert Succumb. In the case of the Overt Succumb, there is an obvious selection of surrender, which is exactly what it appears to be. The Covert Succumb on the other hand is merely a diversion or ploy to avoid domination.

DST – Step 4, Selecting an Optimum Strategy

Finally, you should get a client to decide which is the best, or preferred, option under various circumstances and to give the reasons why. Clients should be especially encouraged to look at the long term implication or consequences of each strategy as a part of their explanation. It is important that they are able to freely select the most appropriate solution at the time, taking current circumstances into account. If needed, steer them away from the idea of a single preferred strategy for all problems, at all times.

An ideal response to a bank robber might well be to give chase and apprehend him, providing you are a fit and healthy young man. This would not be the most sensible approach for an elderly lady. It might not even be appropriate for our healthy young man if the robber were carrying a shotgun, or pointing a pistol at the head of a hostage. The cashier's response would depend on such considerations, as well as the safety of customers and the long term reputation of the bank.

The process should be continued until the client feels there is no further benefit to be gained, or he/she has a realization and has derived a definite benefit from the technique. In any case, this can be a useful little game clients can practice at any time as an amusement, which may help them to restore or improve their problem solving ability. The end point of the technique should be someone who is able to review any given situation and freely choose the optimum strategy for the occasion

Dark Serpent Successes

One Solution Begets Another

We were discussing how the staff in a jeweler's shop should react in an emergency and the dark serpent was described as a means of selecting an optimum strategy. One of the staff said that in the event of a robbery she would stand back and let the intruders help themselves. She could see no point in risking injury by interfering.

Her boss responded by suggesting they should ensure that everything should be kept on display in the window rather than held inside the shop. This would make it difficult for prospective thieves to collect enough valuable merchandise to make it worth their while. By combining these two strategies they were able to reduce the risk of injury to staff by removing the possibility of a successful robbery. Their insurance company was very pleased with the new approach. Incidentally, the new arrangement was more attractive to prospective customers who could now see the whole range of jewelry at a glance.

Commuting Fears

A 35 year-old solicitor, who worked in the City, lived in central London a couple of miles from the office. After the 7th July 2005 bombings he became scared of traveling into the City on the public transport system. He looked at his options and came to the conclusion he could either work from home, cycle to work, walk to work or take a taxi. It was too far to walk, he didn't fee safe on a bicycle so he chose to travel by taxi and work from home whenever he could. He was single and well paid so he felt he could afford this solution.

When engaged with exploring the dark serpent's range of strategies, he said he would be quite prepared to travel out of the City to visit his mother at the weekends. His reasoning was that he would be: "Traveling away from danger zone and the tube would not be quite so crowded on a Sunday morning." We didn't question his logic—it made sense to him. At the weekend he tried out this idea and over the next few weeks grew accustomed to the convenient low-cost option and soon abandoned his need for taxis. He is now a regular commuter once more.

International Aid Agency

An international aid agency which operates in many of the more troublesome part of the world has developed an internal emergency response program. Their directors, senior managers and security staff are trained to deal with incidents that might affect the welfare of their staff or impede their operations.

Members of the emergency response teams participate in regular dark serpent exercises every six months. These exercises are used as a vehicle for applying group thinking to develop solutions for imaginary but plausible problems they might have to deal with. Their level of competence is impressive. In recent years they have had to deal with numerous real life events which have included suicide bombers, hurricanes, typhoons, a tsunami, earthquakes, arson attacks, riots, demonstrations and a kidnapping.

A Chocoholic

A rather well proportioned lady applied the dark serpent process to her apparently insatiable appetite for sweets in general and chocolate in particular. She altered and re-labeled the process to suit her particular type of problem. For her the dark serpent became the "Evil Chocolate Snake" and she had to avoid being bitten by this monster. The result of this twist of logic was the development of a whole range of chocolate avoidance strategies. If pretending it wasn't there didn't work she could avoid contact, run away, throw it in the waste bin, get someone else to eat it or call for help.

A wide range of options improved her chances of addressing what for her was a regularly occurring dilemma. She jokingly remarked: "To misquote Shakespeare, 'To eat or not to eat, that is my question.'"

It's not surprising that Restabilization may seem reminiscent of CISD to some at first glance, because they are both effective treatments for similar conditions. On closer inspection I hope you may begin to realize there are similarities which explain that first impression, but at the same time there are several distinctions which separate them.

Both of these treatment methods were born out of practical experience rather than developed through academic research in an artificial laboratory environment. The basic principles of CISD were originally evolved from Jeffrey Mitchell's experience whilst working as a paramedic serving the public at large. Restabilization was a by-product of the author's work as a disaster recovery and emergency management specialist operating in the cut and thrust of the commercial world where the emphasis was on simple cost effective solutions to extraordinary problems.

Whereas Dr. Jeffrey Mitchell was prompted by his own reactions to a particularly traumatic incident, the author's stimulus was noticing the need in others and watching various counselors' subsequent attempts to deal with those needs. The outcomes were very variable which suggested the need for a more effective standardized approach.

CISD defines a critical incident as:

"An event which is outside the usual range of experience and challenges one's ability to cope. The critical incident has the potential to lead to a crisis condition by overwhelming one's usual psychological defenses and coping mechanisms."

Whilst we have not specifically laid down a definition of what we refer to as the trigger event we would accept this definition as perfectly valid.

Restabilization is a four-step process which is complete in itself, requiring no further treatment. CISD on the other hand seems to include a multi-faceted approach involving primary, secondary and tertiary care.

According to Heath Sommer:

> "Everly and Mitchell (2000) define crisis intervention as "the natural operational corollary of the conceptualization of the term crisis ... crisis intervention may be thought of as an urgent and acute psychological first aid" (p.212). Further, the authors hold that such defined crisis intervention should be immediately implemented, performed in close proximity to the source of the trauma, be in line with the expectations of the recipient (i.e., the authors seem to assume that trauma recipients expect an acute problem-focused intervention), be short (one to three sessions), but simple (i.e., directive, solution focused interventions rather than dynamic, REBT based, etc)."
> (http://www.heathsommer.com/13.html)

Restabilization is similar in its approach with the principal exception that we have a definite number of sessions rather than the one to three of CISD. However, the anticipated outcome from either treatment is similar; the recovery of the recipient's ability and confidence to cope with future problems.

From what I have read about CISD, it appears to be aimed at group therapy and uses seven phases which are covered in sequence. In Restabilization this has been reduced to four sessions; each with a particular objective and outcome. From the recipient's point of view, we would assume progress through the seven

phases of CISD is similar to that obtained in Restabilization where we recognize four milestones on the road
towards full recovery. Another subtle difference is that
the sessions in Restabilization are 'labeled', so the client is aware of the milestones. Whereas, we assume,
the transition from one phase to another within the
CISD process is often quite seamless and the recipient
is not made aware of details such as their current level
of progress.

We also notice that CISD appears to depend upon
establishing good relationships and particular roles in
connection with the work to come. On the other hand
Restabilization uses a 'muzzled' technique in which the
counselor relies entirely on effective communication
within a safe space. The character and personality of
the counselor is not regarded as an asset to be ex-
ploited,   their   expertise   is   self-evident   in   the
unemotional and professional approach which they
adopt. This does require specific training to develop the
ability to stick to the rules of the process under all circumstances. It is not enough for the practitioner to be
familiar with the process: with Restablization the practitioner must be capable of sticking to the associated
rules of counseling. That capability does need to be developed   by   going   through   the   drills   which   we
recommend.

CISD allows for sessions of anything up to three
hours. In our opinion such lengthy sessions can lead to
over-running and going past the point of temporary relief which can usually be achieved within an hour, or
less, when working with individuals; in a group setting
this might become anything up to ninety minutes but
rarely more. A key characteristic of the Restabilization
process is the recognition of an end point which is
based upon the client's indicators. Good indicators are
a sign of temporary relief and tell us when it is best to
end the session and allow the client to enjoy their

achievement and improved condition. If we continue a session beyond this end point the chances are that the client's condition will deteriorate because they may fell overwhelmed by the process. They will feel that we are simply asking too much of them when they would prefer to rest on their laurels and relax for a while. They have reached a pleasure moment which we should allow them to enjoy rather try to press on to the next stage. Pleasure moments are rare enough without being forced to ignore them simply because the bullying counselor wants to get on with their job.

Both techniques recommend delivery within 24—72 hours of the trigger incident. In this regard they are both in accord.

Both techniques use a structured approach, providing a roadmap which helps participants see the light at the end of the tunnel leading towards an achievable holistic recovery.

Aspect	Restabilization	CISD
# Clients	1 or group	groups
# of Sessions	4	1 to 3
Phases	4	7
Phase Transitions	Discrete	Seamless
Counselor	Use Counselor's Code (Chap. 8)	Requires rapport building
Session Length	1 hour max uses end points	3 hours max
Best delivered	First 24-72 hrs	First 24-72 hrs
Structured approach	Yes	Yes

Fig. 10-1 Restabilization and CISD

Glossary of Terms

This glossary contains a definition of all the specialized terms used in the Guide, together with an expanded explanation of the Code for Counselors.

Conscious Mind

The conscious mind is the analytical, thinking level of a person's mind, which a person is normally aware of. This level of the mind is subject to a person's free will, although this of course does not rule out the existence of intrusive thoughts.

End Point

The end point of a session or a process is when the session or process objectives have been met and the client has positive indicators about the situation. It is the moment when the session or process is complete and should be ended, with the client's agreement. Positive indicators from the client are a signal that the end point has been reached.

Neutral Attitude

The counselor should show no hint of antagonism, fear, anger or any other emotion, no implied judgment or criticism. An impartial acceptance of the client's own "universe" makes them feel safe and free to discuss their innermost feelings. If this sense of security is compromised, the client will tend to withdraw from the counselor and the session. The situation can be repaired using the Session Recovery starting on p. 71.

Partial Acknowledgment

A partial acknowledgement is used to indicate that you have received and understood what you have just been told but the subject is not necessarily complete. It is an invitation for the client to continue. In its bluntest form it might be "I understand but is there more to tell?" or "What happened after that?" More commonly it will simply be "Uh huh" or "Mm hmm."

Positive Indicators

Positive indicators are the symptoms displayed by the client when they feel they have made significant progress and are ready to end the session or process. These indications include:

　　a) a smile,
　　b) a statement of feeling good and not bothered by the incident, indicating a degree of relief,
　　c) a willingness to go out and face the world.

Reaction line

A record which traces the variation over time of a person's reaction towards a specific type of event or situation; normally kept to demonstrate their progress during a counseling program.

Restimulate/Restimulation

Whenever someone is reminded, directly or indirectly, of a previously painful experience, their previous subconscious reactions (or mis-emotions) will also return and they become upset without any obvious, current cause and may then seek to justify or explain their discomfort, or find someone or something to blame.

Session

The counseling session is the formally defined period when counseling is under way. There are strict rules of conduct for when a counselor and client are together "In Session"—see the Code for Counselors. Whatever is said during a session is utterly confidential. In the ideal person-centered session, the length is not arbitrarily controlled by the clock (i.e., a prescribed 50 minutes) but allows the client to reach a natural end point.

Subconscious Mind

The subconscious is the level of a person's mind that is not under the control of their free will, and which exerts an influence over their thoughts, actions and reactions.

A person is normally unaware of the influences exerted by the subconscious mind and so their conscious mind will attempt to rationalize and "explain" the resulting behavior in a way that appears to make sense.

Symptoms

The indications of a crisis reaction may include any combination of one, or more, of the following symptoms;

- Increased lethargy, or tiredness

- Extra tension

- A sense of excitement

- A higher accident, or error rate

- Anger

- Acting disorganized, disoriented or withdrawn

A person may experience any of these symptoms to a greater or lesser degree. It is, of course, important to distinguish between tiredness as a reaction to stress and tiredness due to lack of sleep. It is worth asking whether the client has had sufficient sleep, and to ask whether their attention is on a particular problem which may have no relevance to the matter in hand. We are looking for abnormal changes in personal behavior which result from stress rather than normal fluctuations in response to current circumstances.

Trigger Event

There is a delicate balance between the intention to complete the action of experiencing a past trauma and the intention not to experience it. This balance can be upset when something happens that reminds a person of the past trauma. Specifically, this happens when there is some similarity of theme or content between what is going on now and what happened in the traumatic incident. It could be any type of sensory input (e.g. sight, smell, sound, etc.) or spoken words.

Unknowable

The term Unknowable is used to describe a situation which the subconscious mind is unwilling to confront as a realistic possibility. When forced to meet such a situation, the subconscious mind may still refuse to deal with it, resulting in a reaction of "no action".

Appendix

Sources of Information and Assistance

There are many variants on the approach described here and a large number of therapists and counselors who could prove useful after a disaster. For more information about counseling, counselors and counseling courses in the UK, you could contact the British Association for Counseling and Psychotherapy (BACP).

BACP House
15 St. John's Business Park,
Lutterworth, Leicestershire, LE17 4HB
Tele: 0870 443 5252
Website: www.bacp.co.uk

If we miss the window, when the "victim" still has the trigger event in restimulation, we must resort to some form of regression or retrospection therapy. The most effective of these therapies is Traumatic Incident Reduction (TIR), which should only be delivered by a therapist who has been fully trained in the technique. TIR is described in *Beyond Psychology: An Introduction to Metapsychology*, 3rd Ed. by Frank A. Gerbode, M.D.

You can learn more about TIR practitioners and services in your region through the Traumatic Incident Reduction Association (TIRA). Their website can be found at www.tir.org

Bibliography

The following books may prove to be of interest to the reader of this work.

Bisbey, S., & Bisbey, L. (2001). *Brief Therapy for Post-Traumatic Stress Disorder.* Chichester, UK: Wiley Press.

Byron, K., & Mitchell,S. (2002). *Loving What Is.* New York: Harmony Books.

Chalmers, D. (1996). *The Conscious Mind.* Oxford, UK: Oxford University Press.

Dattilio, F & Freeman, A. (2007). *Cognitive-Behavioral Strategies in Crisis Intervention*: 3rd Edition. New York: Guilford Press.

De Bono, E. (1999). *New Thinking for the New Millennium.* London, UK: Viking.

Doherty, G.W. (2007). Crisis Intervention Training for Disaster Workers: An Introduction. Ann Arbor: Loving Healing Press.

Dryden, W., & DiGiuseppe, R. (1990). *A Rational Emotive Therapy Primer.* Champaign, IL: Research Press.

Dryden, W., & Neenan, M. (2006). *Rational Emotive Behaviour Therapy - 100 Key Points and Techniques.* London, UK: Routledge.

Dugas, M., & Robichaud, M. (2006). *Cognitive-Behavioral Treatment for Generalized Anxiety Disorder: From Science to Practice.* New York: Routledge.

Gerbode, F.A. (1995). *Beyond Psychology: An Introduction to Metapsychology, 3rd Ed.* Menlo Park: IRM Press.

Gerbode, F.A. (2005) "Reality and the Person-Centered Approach" in *AMI/TIRA Newsletter,* (ISSN 1555-0818) Vol. 2, No. 2. Ann Arbor: AMI/TIRA.

Ilbury, C., & Sunter, C. (2001). *The Mind of a Fox.* Cape Town, South Africa: Human & Rousseau / Tafelberg.

Moody, R. (1975) *Life After Life: The Investigation of a Phenomenon-Survival of Bodily Death.* London, UK: Harper.

Roberts, A. (2000). *Crisis Intervention Handbook: Assessment, Treatment & Research.* New York: Oxford University Press.

Seligson, B. (1987) *Crisis Intervention: Concepts and Approaches.* Thesis (M.A.) Yellow Springs, OH: Antioch University.

Shine, B. (1991). *Mind Magic.* London, UK: Bantam Press.

Skinner, R., & Cleese, J. (1993) *Life and How to Survive It.* London, UK: Methuen.

Volkman, M. (2005). *Life Skills: Improve the Quality of Your Life with Metapsychology.* Ann Arbor, MI: Loving Healing Press.

Volkman, V. (2005). *Beyond Trauma: Conversations on Traumatic Incident Reduction, 2nd Ed.* Ann Arbor, MI: Loving Healing Press.

Volkman, V. (2006). *Critical Incident Stress Management and Traumatic Incident Reduction: A Synergistic Approach.* Ann Arbor, MI: Loving Healing Press.

Walen, S., DiGiuseppe, R., & Dryden, W. (1992). Practitioners' guide to rational emotive therapy. New York: Oxford University Press.

Wilson, C. (1984). *The Psychic Detectives*. London, UK: Pan Books.

Wright, R. (2001). *Non-zero: The Logic of Human Destiny*. New York: Pantheon.

Index

Exclusive offer for readers of *Coping with Crisis*

Share the power of Loving Healing Press Books
Order direct from the publisher with this form and save!

Order Form – 15% Discount Off List Price!

Ship To:

_____
Name

☐ **VISA**　☐ **MasterCard**　☐ check payable to
Loving Healing Press

_____
Address

_____　_____/_____
Card #　**Expires**

_____
Address

_____
Signature

_____ _____
City　**State**

Coping with Crisis _____ x $17.00 = _____

Beyond Trauma, 2nd Ed _____ x $19.50 = _____

_____
District　**Country**　**Zip/Post code**

Life Skills _____ x $14.50 = _____

_____
Daytime phone #

Subtotal = _____

Residents of Michigan: 6% tax = _____

_____
email address   (in case of difficulty)

Shipping charge (see below) _____

Your Total$_____

Shipping price _per copy_ via:

☐ Priority Mail (+ $3.50)　☐ Int'l Airmail (+ $5)　☐ USA MediaMail/4th Class (+ $2)

Fax Order Form back to (734)663-6861 or
Mail to LHP, 5145 Pontiac Trail, Ann Arbor, MI 48105

CPSIA information can be obtained
at www.ICGtesting.com
Printed in the USA
LVHW091605231218
601536LV00002B/236/P

9 781932 690415